You Bantering Me?

You Bantering Me?

CHRIS HUGHES

CORONET

First published in Great Britain in 2018 by Coronet
An Imprint of Hodder & Stoughton
An Hachette UK company

1

A CIP catalogue record for this title is
available from the British Library

Hardback ISBN 9781473679665
Trade Paperback ISBN 9781473679672
eBook ISBN 9781473679689

Typeset in Adobe Garamond Pro by Palimpsest Book Production Ltd, Falkirk, Stirlingshire

Printed and bound in Great Britain by Clays Ltd, St Ives plc

Hodder & Stoughton policy is to use papers that are natural,
renewable and recyclable products and made from wood grown in
sustainable forests. The logging and manufacturing processes are expected
to conform to the environmental regulations of the country of origin.

Hodder & Stoughton Ltd
Carmelite House
50 Victoria Embankment
London EC4Y 0DZ

www.hodder.co.uk

You Bantering Me?

Prologue

'Hi, is that Chris?'

'Yes.'

'Oh hi, I'm calling from ITV. Just to say that we'd love you to be one of the bombshells on *Love Island* this year.'

'Seriously?'

'Seriously.'

• • • • •

Shit.

1

Meet the Family

My mum said to me recently, 'Chris, what on earth are you writing a book for? You're only twenty-five!' But honestly, I feel like I've got so much to say.

I haven't even been in the public eye for a year yet but so much has happened and a lot has been written about me.

Things have been said that I haven't had a chance to explain or defend, and now it's time.

So here it is, my story, from my early years to my first love, right up to *Love Island* and beyond. I really hope you enjoy it. Love, Chris.

• • • • •

Let's get my younger years covered first so you can find out a bit about my background. I grew up in the Cotswolds in south-central England, which has got a reputation for being really posh and countrified, and also for being home to a lot of politicians, royals and celebrities. There is definitely that element to it but to me it was just home, and a bloody great place to grow up.

I've got four older brothers and, as the youngest, I did get pretty spoiled, which I loved. My two eldest brothers, James and Will, are twins. Will is eight minutes older than James and they were born five weeks prematurely. You wouldn't know it to look at them because they're pretty solid guys. They're forty and James works in farming and Will has his own sports shop and embroidery company.

My brother Tom is thirty-seven and he used to be a furniture restorer, but he now works in social media. He looked after my social media while I was on *Love Island*, which was very useful. I haven't properly thanked him for it yet actually, but I don't know what I would have done without him. And finally there's Ben, who's a year older than me. He's a proper farm boy, and as well as helping run the family farm, he is a gamekeeper and also has a business selling gamekeeping supplies.

My brothers have been really good role models and they've always looked after me. Will especially. He's like the golden boy and the most responsible one of us. I was probably closest to him growing up, and in a way I still am.

James, Will and Tom have got a different dad to Ben and me because my mum had been married once before she met my dad, but we never call ourselves half-brothers. They're my brothers through and through and we think the world of each other.

Most of my brothers are settled down now. James is married with a daughter called Grace, Will has a daughter called Tabitha but isn't married, Tom is married but hasn't got kids, and Ben and I aren't married. Yet.

We're a bit of a mixture when it comes to looks and personality and everyone jokes about me being adopted because I don't look anything like the other boys. Will, James and Tom are pretty similar in some ways because they're all quite sensible, and Ben and I should be more alike because we're so close in age, but we're really not.

James is the quietest and he keeps himself to himself. He's not the most social person you'll ever meet and he mainly concentrates on work. Will is really friendly and he's like the number one son of the family. We always joke that he's Mum's favourite. He's really thoughtful, helpful and generous and if anyone ever needs a chat he's there.

Tom is very opinionated and he's the most outspoken out of all of us. And definitely one of the most intelligent. He's quite chilled and laid-back and pretty sociable. And finally Ben is just . . . Ben. He lives by himself and he loves having his mates round to his or going out with them at weekends. He's pretty lazy but he thinks he works really hard. He only really works hard over the winter, and then he does as little as possible in the summer.

I wouldn't say any of us are properly shy but I've always been the loudest one. Even as a baby, according to my parents.

My parents are brilliant and they brought us up well. My dad works hard and he's a really nice guy. He's stubborn, and I've definitely got my stubbornness from him. We share a lot of personality traits and like me he often says whatever's in his head if he's riled up. I reckon I'm more like him than my mum in a lot of ways. He's always been a great example to me because he keeps his head down, gets on with things and doesn't complain.

My mum looks out for all of us boys and she always knows when something is up with one of us without us having to say anything. She can tell when we're not quite feeling ourselves. We're very close and although I don't always listen, she does give great advice. She's a strong woman – she probably had to be looking after five sons – but she's also very kind and caring.

· · · · ·

I was supposed to be born in Oxford Hospital like all my brothers were, but it was snowing like crazy when my mum went into labour with me and the roads were so bad it was impossible for my parents to drive that far.

My mum was convinced I was going to arrive any minute so they rushed to the nearest hospital, which was in Chipping Norton. Just as they arrived everything stopped and Mum's contractions slowed down, so my dad ended up walking her around the entire town to try to get things going again. Trust me to make them wait. Even now I'm not very good at being on time.

I was eventually born at 5.35 p.m. on 22 December 1992 and I weighed 8lbs 5½ozs so I was a pretty big baby. Mind you, Ben was a 10lb-er so I was probably a breeze after him.

I'm sure my mum, Val, wished I was a girl when I was born. I reckon she had a fifth child just in case, but she denies it. After four boys she must have been pretty hopeful. Thankfully she didn't ever dress me up in girls' clothes or anything, but I was a bit of a mummy's boy. We've always had a tight relationship and even now she's one of the first people I'll turn to if I need help. I get on really well with my dad Paul too, but Mum is usually the first person I'll call.

I would say I was a good kid generally but my parents would disagree. Apparently I screamed the place down when they dipped my head in the water at my christening. Probably because they made me wear a full-length white christening gown and I looked like a bride. The photos are awful. My dad said I cried from the moment we walked in the church until we left. Can you blame me?

But I also had my funny moments. Apparently in the summer after I first learnt to walk I liked wandering around naked outside wearing just my wellies. Mum would try to put clothes on me and I'd refuse. Maybe I was getting into practice for *Love Island*? I also used to get loads of words wrong. I said 'fricken' instead of 'chicken', 'fartridge' instead of 'partridge' and I once told someone I was going to 'Porchicool' instead of 'Portugal'. I also used to talk to my mum about 'Phil' a lot (William Shakespeare). When I was around four my mum asked me why I used so much toilet paper and I replied, 'When you do a poo as big as a chicken you have to use that much.' All in all I was quite a strange child.

I was definitely a handful and apparently I had terrible tantrums when I was really little. I would be fine one minute and then I would totally kick off and I was uncontrollable. There didn't seem to be a pattern to it and sometimes I didn't even need a reason to start screaming. I was basically a little shit.

My mum couldn't get to the bottom of why I was being so awful, and why my behaviour was so erratic. She couldn't see a reason behind the way I reacted, and she knew things couldn't go on the way they were. She had four other kids to look after and she was spending so much time on me trying to help me, the others maybe didn't get as much attention as they needed.

She didn't ever mind looking after me, but I worry it was pretty draining for her sometimes.

She took me to a paediatrician and he told her that I had a behavioural problem and that she'd have to learn to deal with it. He suggested that when I had tantrums she should sit down with me facing away from her and hold on to me tightly until I stopped screaming. She tried it over and over again and it didn't help, funnily enough. I just got more and more wound up and angry.

She was at the end of her tether and she wasn't getting any help or support from the doctors, so she decided to have me allergy tested to see if there was something that was causing me to lash out. When the results came back she discovered that I was allergic to just about everything she was feeding me. My mum is sensitive to certain foods – with her they make her bloat and feel tired, but it seemed to affect me mentally rather than physically.

Mum stopped feeding me anything with E numbers and dairy products and only gave me completely natural foods. After a while she started reintroducing certain foods really slowly to see if I could tolerate them, but anything that had colourings in it was a total no-no.

When I eventually went to nursery when I was four they had to make sure I didn't have any food that contained colourings, so I wasn't allowed things like ketchup or Smarties like the other kids were. I was always a bit different like that. I had to be really careful with sugar too. I got quite hyper and I had a few anger problems if I ate too much sweet stuff.

To be fair I must have been a bit of a nightmare. My mum was probably thinking 'Why did I ever have a fifth child?' I could definitely be a bit of an arsehole. Can you say that about a young child? From the sound of things I really was.

Thankfully I grew out of the allergies when I hit my teens and they didn't have any kind of effect on me physically. I was just as healthy as other children my age, and strangely I didn't take my bad moods out on strangers. Apparently I was only really badly behaved at home. My teachers were always telling my mum what a charming little boy I was, and how well behaved I had been, which must have been very annoying for her. I only had meltdowns at home, and when I did I only wanted Will to comfort me. He was always the one I asked for when I was on one.

I was always trying to get Ben into trouble too. He was much better behaved than me and clearly I didn't like it. When he was five he was asked to be a pageboy for some friends of my parents and before we even got into the church I was being a little git. I tried to climb a tree in my smart clothes and I had a massive tantrum when my mum tried to stop me.

Ben was a little angel during the ceremony, but when we were driving to the reception I told him to get out of his 'funny clothes'. He was wearing a morning suit and I didn't like it, and I gave him such a hard time he ended up stripping off in the back of the car and then refused to get dressed again.

When we arrived at the reception I threw another massive tantrum because I didn't want to go inside, and my dad was so sick of me he ended up driving me all the way home, which was over an hour away, and leaving me with my granddad. I was as strong-willed then as I am now.

I think because I was the youngest I thought I deserved more than anyone else. I had a proper sense of entitlement.

If I didn't get what I wanted when I was really young I used to scream the place down and I think it was easier for my parents to give in to me. I don't know if I can blame that on being spoiled when I was growing up but I definitely was. I always wanted my own way. I was a sweet-looking kid and I looked like butter wouldn't melt, but when I have a family of my own, I wouldn't want a child like me!

I stopped being as difficult around the time I finished primary school, around ten or eleven. The outbursts stopped and I handled things much better. I guess that's all part of growing up and I became more conscious of how I was acting. I realised that I wasn't just showing my mum up when I started ranting. I was showing myself up too.

I loved Christmas growing up. Because my birthday is on 22 December I was never at school for it. I'd have the come-down after my birthday but then I'd have Christmas to pick me back up again. The only annoying thing was that I'd often get given joint presents by people. I'd get given a gift from a relative and they'd be like 'This is for Christmas too.' Considering I was a bit of a brat generally, I was strangely fine about it. I wasn't a very materialistic kid, and I didn't expect lavish parties.

Having said that, I remember one year I had a party on a thing called the Big Red Party Bus. It was a double decker bus (funnily enough) and it had loads of games and a ball pit on it. All my mates came round and we piled on and I had a brilliant time, but I didn't love the fact that all the attention was on me.

I've never enjoyed people making a big fuss over my birthday. I don't like people having to go out of their way to make me feel special. I'm happy waking up on my birthday and chilling and then going for a nice meal with a few mates in the evening. I would feel really under pressure if I had a party now. You can't enjoy yourself because you're worrying about whether everyone else is having a good time or not. I would rather chill, or enjoy someone else's party, because then there's no stress. I went to Thailand for my twenty-first for two weeks rather than have a party. Ben had a big do for his and Mum and Dad offered me one too but I was much happier to go away.

It's weird that I'm on TV in front of millions of people now because I wasn't the loudest kid in class growing up. I was always confident but I didn't go out of my way to get attention or be in the limelight and I didn't need everyone to know who I was.

I'd happily talk to anyone one on one but I hated it if I was made to stand up in front of a group of people and talk.

I've done talks to hundreds of people now and it freaked me out the first time I had to do it, but because I had to do it I had no choice but to face my fears. If someone asked me to do a speech at their wedding now I would feel fine about it because I've had some practice, but a year ago I would have felt well out of my comfort zone. I'm still happy to tuck myself away without anyone knowing what I'm doing and for no one to talk about me, but I am more comfortable with large groups now.

My mum always gave my brothers and me sacks filled with presents at Christmas. And bless her; she still does that for Ben and me now. She often got the two of us the same presents when we were young, but she'd get them in different colours to stop us arguing over them. I remember us getting a little blue toy tractor with pedals, which was a lot of fun. Well, I say 'us' but it was Ben's really. He'd let me sit on it every now and again if he was feeling generous.

I used to get given a lot of football shirts, which I really liked, and when I got older I always asked for money. That way you can buy what you like with it, can't you? That's all stopped now, sadly.

My family always went to midnight mass at the church across the road when I was young, and then we'd be allowed to open one present when we got back because it was technically already Christmas Day.

I love the feeling of waking up on Christmas Day because everyone is in such a good mood. We always have lots of family round for lunch. Everyone gets together on Boxing Day too, and there is always good sport on TV and we play silly games. It's like a big celebration with my extended family. My dad is usually thinking about work 24/7 but he relaxes and lets his hair down for once, and it's nice to see that. We've always got the fire on and the house gets roasting hot, to the point where we have to open the windows to get some air in.

It's not just Christmas that's my favourite time of the year. I love the whole of winter. I like wearing more clothes and feeling cosy. Chilling in front of the TV when it's cold outside is so simple but one of the nicest things you can do.

Considering we're such a big family we get on really well. My brothers are like my mates and we'll all go and play snooker and have a few drinks together like a normal group of lads. We all really enjoy spending time together and it's really easy-going. None of us bicker or fall out. We'll have a bit of banter and take the piss out of each other a bit, but there are never any full-on arguments.

My extended family is huge. I've got so many cousins and

second cousins I lose count. But we never have any of that awkwardness that can sometimes go with family gatherings or parties. And I don't dread them. I actually look forward to them.

I haven't got any grandparents left and that's a real shame because I didn't ever get to the point where I could appreciate them. My dad's mum passed away before I was one and my mum's mum passed away when I was four. My mum's dad passed away when I was ten, and my dad's dad died when I was around twenty. He got ill and died really quickly and I wish I'd had a chance to get to know him better. He ended up in hospital on a lot of medication and it really affected his brain. My dad would go in to visit him and he'd ask him all these questions, like if he'd signed for stone at the quarry. He hadn't worked in a quarry for about twenty years at that point. I think that was really hard on my dad.

Isn't it weird how the mind works? My granddad didn't know where he was or what was going on in those moments but his mind had rolled back to the past and he could remember things from decades ago so clearly. It just goes to show how much we store. We forget about so much of our lives but it's all still in there somewhere and finds its way out without us realising.

All my granddad wanted was to be at home when it got near the end, so they moved his bed downstairs and set up the hospital equipment there. The doctors told all of the family to go and see him and it was so sad. I went with my dad and it was really hard to see him looking so unwell but I was so happy that he got to pass away in his house, which is what he wanted more than anything.

When things like that happen you can't help but question what life is all about, can you? I am definitely guilty of thinking about things too much sometimes, and you might have noticed I quite often go off on tangents. I can't help myself. I think I've just got a really active imagination or something.

After I lost my granddad I started wondering why someone's body can work for ninety years and then it suddenly decides it can't any more? And why do some people live longer than others?

I do believe in God and I do believe in the afterlife. I always have and I always will. I don't think anything influenced that; it's how I've felt since I was a kid.

I don't fear death because I know I'll have another life at some point, if you know what I mean? I think we live for ever and we keep coming back as different things. No one knows for sure what really happens but why not look on the bright side?

· · · · ·

On a lighter note, I really enjoyed going on holiday with my family in my younger years. The first time we went away it was to Bournemouth when I was nearly three, and apparently I was a total nightmare (no surprise there). I picked up a handful of sand and threw it at my dad and it all went in his face. He was not happy. Weirdly, I remember it quite well. I thought it was really funny but I got properly told off.

My parents booked quite a posh hotel and they had to have meals in shifts. I'd kick off at the dinner table and either Mum or Dad had to look after me in the room so the other one could eat.

My dad's not at all fussed about going on holiday and he'd

be happy if he never went abroad again, but he used to take us away so we could experience it. He's not great with hot weather and he's not used to sitting around doing nothing, but at least it meant he was forced to relax a bit. We went abroad every two years or so, and in between we'd go on holiday in the UK, to places like Cornwall and the south-west of Devon.

I used to go away with my mum, dad and Ben because my other brothers were a bit too old to go on holiday with their parents. We went to Spain and Portugal a lot because the flights are short, so there was less chance of me making the plane journey a pain in the arse.

One of my favourite holidays was in Majorca when I was about five. That's when I learnt to swim. I'd always swum with armbands and all of a sudden I was in the water without them. I remember flapping my arms and thinking 'Hang on, I'm not sinking.' It was a surreal feeling.

I'm not a great swimmer now and it's certainly not something I do for fun. I know it's good for fitness but I find it annoying. The worst thing was when we had to do it at school in front of everyone. If you were good you were allowed up the deep end and if you weren't you had to stay in the shallow end. I was somewhere in between but I thought it was mean. And who wants to have to strip off in front of their entire class as a teenager? It can scar you for life.

Some of my earliest memories are from that Majorca holiday. We always used to eat in the same restaurant every night and this waiter called Carlos always served us. I also burned my feet so badly I had to go to hospital. We were walking along the pavement and I took my shoes off and then I ran away from my parents. It was roasting hot and my feet were soft because I was so young and they swelled up and blistered. It was agony.

As most people know, I grew up on a farm, and even though I went to school in the middle of the Cotswolds not many of the other kids I knew came from farming backgrounds. I was in a very small percentage. I wouldn't say growing up on a farm was massively different to anyone else's childhood, but I did enjoy going to my mates' houses because they were 'normal' in my eyes, and I always thought that was quite fun.

Our farm is made up of five buildings surrounding the main yard. One of the buildings is where we keep all of the machinery and there's a barn where all the cows go. We've got another barn that's always full of turkeys before Christmas. My dad breeds them for a hobby and Ben kills, plucks and dresses them, then my mum finishes them off and wraps them and decorates them before we sell them. She gets these really nice trays and wraps them in packaging. Then she puts a big bow on them to make them look pretty. Turkeys don't look the best, do they? But Mum manages to make them look a bit more attractive.

The turkeys go to the same loyal customers every single year and it's something my dad takes real pride in. I have no idea why he does it because they stink. They smell like prawn cocktail crisps, and farming turkeys is not a money-making enterprise. You barely make a penny from it.

I remember a couple of years ago having to chase one round trying to catch it and it flicked a load of shit at me. It splattered all over my face and my brother Ben was wetting himself. I looked at that turkey's face and thought 'I'll feel better about this when I'm eating you.'

We had too many pigs when I was young. We had two

called Sid and Sod who were my favourites. I was about eight when we got them and they were well cute and I used to go and see them all the time. I honestly don't know what happened to them and I don't want to know. One day they just weren't there any more. We've still got a lot of sheep, and then we've got all the fields. Last year we had a field that had fifteen cows and one bull in it. That bull was responsible for impregnating all of those cows. I don't get how one bull can have so much go in him. Can you imagine that pressure? Mind you, he always looked like he had a massive smile on his face.

I always wonder if the cows get jealous that he's kind of dating them all at the same time. What if one of them really fell for him and he's putting it about with all the others? There's nothing to say they don't catch feelings for each other when it's all going on. It doesn't seem right. I don't think my dad thinks that deeply into it though.

I like springtime on the farm best because that's when we have lambing and the calves are born, and that's amazing. All of it's pretty amazing really. I didn't ever think I would follow my dad into the farming world because it didn't feel right for me, but it was a really nice environment to grow up in. I didn't spend my days skipping through fields wearing a straw hat and dungarees like I was in a film or anything, but we had a lot of freedom.

Ben and I had motorbikes from a young age, and then later on my dad got us quad bikes. Can you imagine how cool it was bombing around the fields on those? It got me out and about and I didn't spend much time inside. It would have been criminal if I'd lived somewhere as amazing as that and sat in my bedroom every day.

I've never been a massive gamer and although I had a PlayStation growing up and I liked FIFA, I preferred being outside. When I have a kid there's no way I'll let them sit around playing games all day. Even if they did want to stay inside I'd encourage them to read or get a hobby or watch educational films. It worries me that kids are so addicted to games these days. I get it and there is a reason the industry is worth millions, but it's not healthy.

Ben and I were always playing cops and robbers and running or BMXing when we were young. We were properly active. We were allowed to be kids, whereas kids nowadays are wearing full make-up at twelve or thirteen and worrying about what they look like all the time. I know I sound like an old man but I really hope we can eventually get back to a point where childhood is a more innocent time again instead of children worrying about how many likes they've got on a selfie.

My parents are building another house up on the farm at the moment. My dad's spent twenty years trying to get planning permission and it's finally gone through, so that's all under way and he's really excited about it. We've also got holiday cottages in the village which we rent out. We get a lot of families and hen dos coming to stay and Mum takes care of it all. It's only been trashed once but when it was there was red wine up the walls and mess everywhere and that was a bit of a nightmare.

My dad works his bollocks off every single day. He goes to bed at around 11–11.30 p.m. and his alarm goes off at 6 a.m. He never has a lie-in and he never complains about it. He doesn't sit down during the day because he's always doing something, whether it's working on the farm or doing stuff around the house. He also owns his own electrical firm and employs a cousin of mine. He has found it more tricky to kneel down since having his knee operation.

My dad has always been really strong and healthy but he suffered with Menieres Disease which he had for three years. This is an infection of the inner ear. He was so ill he woke up in the middle of the night and told my mum he thought he was dying. He was really scared, as were all of us.

It got so bad he was throwing up six or seven times a day for months on end. He used to lose his balance all the time too, and he was up on some scaffolding doing some building work on our house one day when he went dizzy and collapsed and threw up everywhere. Thankfully he didn't fall and hurt himself too badly but it could have been really nasty.

It was hoped that the disease would clear up on its own but it didn't. He wasn't allowed to drive in case he felt faint at the wheel and it drove him mad. My dad is someone who doesn't do illness. He's always on the go but that knocked him for six. In the end he had a procedure to poison his ear but left him deaf in that ear.

As well as being on turkey duty and looking after the holiday cottage, Mum does all the accounts for both the farm and the electrical business, so she's not exactly lazy either. They've both instilled a really good work ethic in me and I'm not afraid to knuckle down and get stuff done when I need to. I love my downtime in front of the TV but I always show up when I'm supposed to, and I hate letting people down.

• • • • •

Even though I was tricky at home I loved starting nursery school and I turned out to be quite well behaved there. I was never short of friends and some of the mates I made there are still my closest mates now.

The thing I remember most clearly about nursery was the food. I loved the lasagne and to this day I can still remember how good it tasted. We used to get given milk with malted milk biscuits, and because of that I used to look forward to break-time every day.

After nursery I went to a primary school that was literally 100 yards down the road from where I lived. I could get out of bed late and still have a big cooked breakfast before I went to school. I think most of my early memories are pretty food-based if I'm being honest. I still love a full English to this day.

The scariest thing that happened to me as a kid was on 28 August 2002 (I know that's very precise, but it's a day I'll never forget) when I was ten. Mum took Ben and me out for the day with some friends of ours, Harry and George, and their mum Vanessa.

Mum had been ill for a few days before with what she thought was a virus and she'd even had a day in bed, which was unheard of for her. She didn't feel 100 per cent but she felt well enough to take us to a village called Hidcote, which had a big maze for us to run around in.

Because Mum had a big car she drove us all and I remember us boys laughing and joking on the way there. It was a really hot day and we were all messing around in the maze when Mum all of a sudden took a turn for the worse and started to feel very ill. She said to Vanessa, 'I really don't feel well. I'm going to have to get out of here.'

They managed to find a way out through a hedge and find a place to sit down, but Mum started to feel even worse. We went to find them, not realising anything was wrong, and then Vanessa turned to Ben and me and said, 'Your mum needs to go to hospital. She's not feeling good at all.'

We all bundled into the car and Mum drove us all to the nearest hospital, which was about six miles away in Moreton-in-Marsh. When we arrived Mum went straight to A&E and Vanessa took all of us kids to Budgens to get some lunch. Then we headed to the park to wait for news from Mum.

Mum was given an ECG and then asked to make her way to our regular doctor's surgery, which was about a quarter of a mile away, to wait for the results. They said it wasn't safe for her to drive, so she had no choice but to walk all the way there in the blazing sunshine.

When she arrived the doctor called her in, took one look at her ECG results and said, 'I need to fax this to Cheltenham Hospital for them to look at. I've got a couple more patients to see so if you can sit in the waiting room I'll let you know the outcome as soon as possible.'

Mum took a seat in the empty waiting room and that's the last thing she remembers. When the doctor came out to give her the ECG results he found her slumped over two chairs. He called her name and tried to wake her but she wasn't responding, so he shouted to someone nearby and they helped to get her down on to the floor.

Someone immediately phoned for a paramedic, and in the meantime the doctor worked on my mum for around seven minutes to keep her heart pumping. It wasn't until the paramedics arrived that she came to again.

An ambulance took her straight to Cheltenham Hospital, and in the meantime Vanessa drove us all home. After a lot of waiting we got a phone call saying that Mum had suffered a cardiac arrest. It was such a shock to everyone because she was very slim and fit and healthy and she didn't drink or smoke. She was the last person you would expect something like that to happen to. She was only in her mid-forties and thankfully she hasn't been unwell since and her heart wasn't damaged, but she's been on tablets for high cholesterol ever since.

Mum was in hospital for nine days and I remember going to visit and being so scared that something bad was going to happen again. The doctor told my dad that they genuinely thought they'd lost her when she was lying on the floor of the GP surgery, and that doesn't even bear thinking about.

I can't even think about my mum not being here. I don't treat her with enough respect sometimes, considering how much I love her. I'm really aware that I take her for granted at times, and when I think back to that day and how terrifying it was, it makes me want to show my appreciation more. I don't always do that but I hope she knows how much she means to me.

I think it's because I'm the youngest that we've got such a really strong bond. I also had more problems than my brothers growing up so she looked out for me a lot. I was the last son to leave home and I still like getting her opinions on things. Even though I'm twenty-five I'll always be her baby.

Sometimes I'll ask her about something and she'll want to go really in-depth and talk about it for ages and I'll cut her off because I'm like 'Okay, I've got my answer, that's enough talking for now,' but she wants to make sure I'm all right. I find it easier talking to her via text than face to face sometimes.

Mum is so active and always on the go so all of us have to step in and tell her to calm things down sometimes. She's such a strong woman but she needs to take better care of herself. She'll go to bed after midnight and gets up at 7 a.m., but she says that staying busy and active and helping my dad out is what keeps her going. And of course she's got five sons to look after. I'm probably a full-time job on my own.

The following year something else horrendous happened that I don't think my family will ever get over. My brother James had an amazing three-year-old son called Charlie, and we lost him in really tragic circumstances. I won't go into details out of respect for my brother, but it was an awful time for all of us.

Charlie would have been seventeen now and it still shocks me that he's not here. But we still talk about him a lot and he's still very much a part of our family.

When things are a bit shit, sometimes I think about what James went through when he lost his little boy and nothing compares to it. It makes me appreciate the people I love even more.

The last ten things I bought and why

A bread bin because I needed somewhere to put bread. It's the first one I've ever bought and I felt well proud.

A kitchen roll holder. You can probably guess what that does. It's silver and it matches the bread bin.

A hairdryer. I've never actually owned one before. I did steal one from a hotel room by mistake once but that's the first one I've bought.

A washer dryer. It washes your clothes and dries them too. It's like magic. I don't know how to work it but I'll teach myself.

Coat hangers. I bought 300 wooden ones from Ikea. They cost a fortune.

I did a Marks and Spencer's shop and spent £150, but that did include petrol. I like M&S pizzas. They're like proper ones.

Indian takeaway. I had chicken tikka masala and coconut rice. I have the same every time.

Reebok trainers. I've got a little obsession with them. I like to buy every new pair that comes out.

Dishwasher tablets. Well exciting.

A bottle of water. I get thirsty. I suppose we all do.

2

Night-mare

I had a really nice childhood and I was always aware of that growing up. My mum and dad did everything for us and I was always well looked after and given the opportunity to do whatever I wanted. I played a lot of sport from a young age and looking back I wish I'd just concentrated on one type so I could have been brilliant at one thing instead of good at several. But I guess at least I got to try out a lot of different things. I played rugby, football, tennis, cricket and golf and rode horses, and I loved it all.

I first started riding horses when I was about seven or eight. I had a pony called Nutmeg and she was a proper nutter. I kept her in a field behind our house on the farm. She was really headstrong, but as a result she taught me to be a better rider. Every time I sat on her she would challenge me. We both wanted our own way so it was a real battle of wills. After riding Nutmeg I found it boring if I was given a placid horse to ride instead.

Sadly she got put down when I was about eleven because she was old and unwell. She was struggling with all her limbs and joints. I had to go to school knowing I wasn't going to come home to her. I went to say goodbye to her before I got on the school bus and I was crying my eyes out.

I used to go to Pony Club Camp and do gymkhanas and showjumping, and I'm so lucky I grew up somewhere where I had the opportunity to do all of that, but I kind of hated Pony Club Camp. It wasn't really for me. I only went because I knew my parents wanted me to. It was only five minutes from home so there was no real need for me to camp, and it was hard work because I had to get my horse there every day. In a way it was the start of me being more independent because I was away from home a bit, but I would rather have been out hunting.

I was all right at the showjumping and gymkhanas because I just went for it but, again, I wasn't that into it. I didn't go home with armfuls of rosettes but I was okay. There wasn't a lot of risk involved with showjumping and I preferred the element of fear and the adrenalin you get with hunting.

I got a black Welsh Cob called Rita next. I loved her but she had an even worse attitude than Nutmeg. If I took her out, one day she would be totally fearless and would jump anything, no matter how high. Then I'd take her out the next day and if she didn't fancy going over a jump she'd dig her heels in and she'd refuse to do anything. She was a nightmare. She's always wanted her own way and she often tried to throw me off if I was strict with her, so I had to hold on really tightly.

I had Rita until I was about seventeen and she's still alive and living in the Cotswolds. She's had a couple more homes since I had her and I like to think she's in a field chilling happily.

I've always had female horses and they've always been proper madams, and most of my exes were like that too. I seem to attract those kinds of females. I've definitely met some spirited women in my time.

As a result of having challenging horses I became a pretty fearless rider quite young. If you're going to sit on such a big animal when you're so small you've got to be brave about it.

I once rode a horse at a race yard that hadn't been broken in. She was a little strawberry blonde pony called Lucky. I went out for a canter on her one day and she decided she wanted to speed things up, so we ended up going for a gallop across this field. She was going so fast her front legs buckled underneath her and I ended up flying over her head and landing on the floor. It happened so quickly that I was in total shock.

I could have been really badly injured because she could easily have rolled over on top of me or kicked me, but somehow I managed to escape totally unhurt. For some reason when you have a riding accident, on the way down you somehow work out how to fall. It's like your body adapts and naturally falls into the shape that will do you the least damage.

That fall didn't put me off riding again or make me nervous about riding. I literally got back in the saddle straight away and it didn't affect me at all. I've fallen off a few times since when I've been going over jumps but I see that as part and parcel of riding. Everyone falls off sometimes, even the professionals, and unless you really damage yourself the best thing to do is get straight back on.

· · · · ·

I always loved the Christmas Eve hunt when I was growing up. It took place in a village called Kineton, which was the next village to where I lived. People used to put tinsel on their horses and it felt really festive and exciting.

One year, when I was about fourteen, I took Rita out alongside one of my friends, Jonathan England, who's now a professional jockey. We were only supposed to be going out for an hour or so but we ended up being out for five hours. We lost track of time and all of a sudden we found ourselves in the middle of this massive forest called Hinchwick Wood.

We were totally lost and a bit worried because we didn't have phones on us, and in the end the organisers had to send out a search party for us. We managed to find our way to the main road and thankfully one of the horse lorries spotted us and picked us up. It was a bit scary but it was one of those days I'll never forget. Even though it was pitch black and freezing and we were wondering if we'd ever get home, I recall it as a really nice Christmassy memory.

I know that hunting is really frowned upon these days and I do totally get that, but I grew up around it so it was like second nature to me and it wasn't something I ever questioned. It's something that's been going on for hundreds of years and it was part and parcel of growing up in the Cotswolds. It wasn't until people started petitioning for a ban that I stopped and thought about it. Obviously I don't hunt any more because the ban has come in, and I guess looking back it feels quite weird that I ever did it.

I still ride as much as I can when I go home. I ride out with a guy called Jonjo O'Neill, who is a racehorse trainer and ex-jockey and lives just near me. Or I'll go with Aidan Coleman and Richie McLernon, who are also jockeys, and one of my best mates Sam Twiston-Davies, who is a jump jockey and his mum, Cathy would take us to nursery school in a cart pulled by a horse called Brian.

Six or seven of the guys from my year at school are professional jockeys now because riding was such a popular thing to do in my area, and even now when I watch racing I want to be there racing with them. I did think about riding professionally when I was younger but because I'm 6ft and weigh twelve and a half stone it was always difficult for me to make the weight. You have to be very slight to be a jockey and it was obvious from quite a young age I was going to be quite tall and pretty well built.

I actually thought about getting my amateur licence before I went on *Love Island*, but it meant a lot of early mornings and hard work and I just didn't have the time to do it. It's something I still think about doing, so when things calm down I might go for it.

I got the opportunity to do some racing when Coral approached me to do some work with them. They knew I was into riding because I've done a lot of interviews about racing, for people like ITV and Ascot Promotions.

They asked if I would be interested in running in a charity race and becoming a kind of brand ambassador for them. It involves me running in a race alongside professional jockeys, probably over a mile, and hopefully winning it. It will be all over their social media in the lead-up and it's a really exciting thing to be a part of.

I'm training three times a week riding at different yards in Surrey and the Cotswolds, and I'm hoping to ride one of the horses that Jonjo trains.

I've got to get down to 11st 7lbs in time for the race, so I've got to lose nine pounds in total. It'll just be a case of watching what I eat, and all the training will help too.

It's incredible to get the opportunity to do something like that. I miss being able to ride as much as I did, so it will be nice to be able to do what I love and call it work.

· · · · ·

The first job I ever had was washing plates at a local pub when I was fourteen. I worked there one or two nights a week and then one day I was asked to take some food out to diners and I thought I was the bollocks. Honestly, I thought I'd properly made it. I was never precious about what kind of jobs I did. I was happy to do anything to make a bit of money so I could go out with my mates at the weekend, or eat out. I've always loved eating out. I would much rather go to a restaurant or pub than cook myself. I went out to eat pretty much every night or lunchtime for five months after I left *Love Island*.

I did help out on our farm too when Dad needed me or when Mum required help during night lambing with the feeding and watering of the ewes, but Ben was always much more into it than me. He's got no qualms about killing and skinning a rabbit or shooting a deer. It doesn't faze him at all, but it's not for me. I've been out shooting and I've shot birds and partridge but it was never something I got seriously into, and I couldn't imagine having to pluck a bird or prepare it for eating. I hate the thought of it.

I worked at Marcella Bayliss' point-to-point yard for a few

years after I left the pub. They kept racehorses that were one step down from National Hunt level, including Earth Summit, in his retirement, winner of the Grand National and the Scottish and Welsh equivalents so I used to ride the horses and muck them out and all that kind of thing. I was a pretty experienced rider, so even though they were incredible horses I could handle them. I was basically an all-round stable lad and it was a good education.

· · · · ·

I was very sociable at school and I was never stuck for friends. Despite that I liked being on my own too, and I could sometimes go off into my own little world. I've always been very happy in my own company. Even now I'm just as comfortable by myself as I am around people.

I was never bullied at school or anything, but I did feel a bit scared about starting high school at the Cotswold School in case I got picked on. You've got people who are six years older than you roaming around, which is pretty intimidating. I needn't have worried because I got on with everyone okay.

My brother Ben was in the year above me so it helped having him there, but it wasn't like he was my big protector or anything. I had quite a lot of mates in his year anyway because I was in the cricket, rugby and football teams for both my year and his year. I played a lot of cricket growing up. I played for Gloucester's youth group and Ben played for Worcestershire and it was a really good experience.

The only time I got really bollocked at secondary school was when my mates and I talked and laughed through a school play when I was in Year 10. One of the kids in the play complained to the scariest teacher in the school and he called us into his classroom and went mad at us. I was put in isolation for a few days, which meant I had to sit with the deputy head and do all my lessons on my own. Apart from that I was pretty well behaved. I was a bit crap at doing my homework but I was never one of those kids who was smoking behind the bike sheds or getting into fights.

Not surprisingly, sport was my strong point the whole way through school. I used to be properly buzzing when I went in knowing I had a game later that day. Aside from sport I liked English, because I fancied my teacher, and I always thought I was good at art, maths and geography.

I liked geography because I liked natural disasters like earthquakes and volcanoes. I went to the Tsunami Museum when I went to Thailand and it was mind-blowing. I find stuff like that so fascinating. Things like tectonic plates and the pyroclastic flows of lava are just ridiculous. I could watch programmes about that kind of thing for hours. I find it so weird that every little thing we do has an effect on the rest of the world. Everything we say and do affects everything else. What I'm saying now could be having an effect on something on the other side of the world. How mad is that?

I didn't always concentrate that well in classes but I did all right in my GCSEs.

I didn't revise for a single one of my exams so when you consider how I did it's really not that bad. I got the worst PE theory score in the history of my school, 13%, but I still got a B in sport because I got 100% in my practical. I was intelligent enough to get decent results without revising so it does make me wonder what I could have achieved if I'd got my head down and studied really hard.

I didn't think I really needed good exam results. My plan

when I was younger was to be some kind of sportsman. I didn't have any firm ideas and I just kind of hoped I'd end up where I wanted to. I'm pretty good at going with the flow and seeing where it leads me.

I always liked the idea of doing something that didn't feel like work, like acting or modelling. That sounds well big-headed, but I don't mean it like that. I just wanted to do something that was fun and didn't feel like a proper job.

It wasn't like I thought I was Brad Pitt or something, but I didn't worry about my looks when I was younger and I guess I always knew I was all-right looking. The only thing I was insecure about was my ears because I thought they were weird. I don't know why because they're still the same shape now and there's nothing wrong with them.

I didn't ever feel hugely self-conscious aside from my ears, and a few people told me I should try modelling, so I guess that also gave me a big confidence boost.

In the end I did an online application for a modelling agency and I got asked to go for a meeting in London. They signed me and shot a portfolio for me and I was put on their books. I didn't think too much about it and just figured that if I got some work it would be a bonus, and if I didn't it wouldn't be the end of the world.

I did modelling for a year or two, from the age of eighteen, but because I was living in the Cotswolds I didn't ever go to any castings, even though I got asked to go to a lot. It would have cost me £60 on the train to get to London and I'd lose a day's work, and to be honest I couldn't be arsed. My agency did ask me to go but if I didn't get the job I would have been down on money and it wouldn't be worth it, so I only took jobs that were offered to me outright.

I did a few magazine shoots for smaller companies, and I did a shoot for a clothing company in Dubai and Wolverhampton Wanderers football club's team wear for their magazine. I also did something for American Crew hair products.

I don't think I had the out-and-out model look that people go for. I wasn't very chiselled or anything, and I think I probably look better and photograph better now. I wasn't ever going to get hired for Prada or Gucci. I was more boy next door. I got a little buzz out of it though, and it was a nice way to get a little bit of money in because the day rates or fees were decent.

I loved seeing the finished shots after I'd done a shoot, and it was cool if I got to see myself in a magazine. I always enjoyed modelling and it was fun, but it was never something I saw myself doing full-time or long-term.

Eventually I stopped doing it because it ended up being more hassle than it was worth. I was working in a solicitors' office at nineteen so it became harder and harder to go to jobs. My boss was really good about letting me have the odd day off but I didn't want to take the piss and end up losing my job.

· · · · ·

I loved my school years so much. I'd drop what I'm doing now in a second if I could go back to my schooldays. It was sick. You had so much freedom. I'd like to go back now and sit in lessons and take exams and not worry, knowing I would be okay in the future. I wish I knew then what I know now; that I'd chill out until twenty-four and then go on *Love Island* and everything would be okay.

Like any kid I went through a few different style phases in my teens. I was a real indie kid in Years 7, 8 and 9. I had quite long hair and I was into bands like the Wombats, the Kooks, Razorlight, the View and the Killers. I wore a lot of skinny clothes but in my opinion nothing really bad. I used to really pluck my eyebrows a lot around that time too, and I remember a female teacher coming up to me one day and saying, 'I really like your eyebrows.' No fourteen-year-old boy wants to hear that. That's when I decided to completely reassess my eyebrow style and let them grow a bit more.

The first time I ever drank I was thirteen or fourteen. I had a pint of cider and I was so drunk I was all over the place. I used to go to camp-outs with mates when I got to around fifteen or sixteen and they were decent fun because we'd get our hands on some alcohol, usually through a mate's older sibling, and we'd get drunk very, very quickly. I didn't ever actually camp because I absolutely hate it, so we called it a camp-out but really we were just going to get boozed in a field. Half the time the police would come and we'd get kicked out and sent home. That's what being a teenager was all about for us.

I had my first kiss on a camp-out when I was about fifteen but I can't remember the girl's name, which is a bit rude. I know it begins with R and she was blonde but that's all I can tell you. I wasn't nervous about it because I was a bit drunk, and I had a proper skip in my step when I went home that night. I thought I was the boy. Was it what I was expecting? I suppose it was really. It feels like a lifetime ago now and yet it was only ten years ago. I like to think I've got a bit better since then.

• • • • •

There was never a time when I suddenly realised I wasn't a kid any more. To be honest I still feel like a kid sometimes now. I don't think many people get to the point where they suddenly think 'Oh yeah, I'm a grown-up.' I keep thinking I'm going to wake up and feel like a proper adult but I never have. I like that though. It's good to stay young.

I don't really remember going through puberty and my voice breaking or anything. I didn't wake up one day with a full beard and a deep voice but I knew things were happening to my body and that I was changing. Hair suddenly appeared and I had some pretty irrational teenage moods (I can't blame those on food colourings).

I also suffered from acne for a while. One day I noticed I had all these spots coming up on my cheeks and I was not happy about it. I tried creams and lotions from the doctor but nothing shifted them. In the end I had to go on a course of antibiotics to get rid of them. I've been lucky that they've never come back majorly. I get the odd spot here and there like everyone, but nothing too bad.

I think it was just an age thing but it did affect my confidence. When you're at school and everyone is seeing you every day you just have to get on with it, but it made me feel very self-conscious. At least girls can cover their spots up with make-up, but as a guy you just have to crack on with it. Blokes should be able to wear make-up if they want to. I wear make-up if I go to an event now, or if I'm on a shoot I always get my hair and make-up done. Every male and female TV presenter you see is wearing make-up, even if it's just a bit of powder to stop them looking shiny. I've got used to it now and I don't even think about it.

I played in a charity football match last year and I knew I

was going to have my photo taken afterwards. I had a shower and got changed and then I went over to the mirror to do my hair and put a bit of powder on. I was worried in case people saw me and said something, but then Calum Best came and stood next to me and he started putting powder on as if it was the most natural thing in the world. And why not? It just smooths your face out. If you'd told me when I was younger I'd wear make-up I probably would have laughed, but I've become more confident in myself and now I get on with doing what's right for me.

It's become more acceptable for boys to wear make-up in everyday life on the whole, and that's how it should be. Who writes these rules anyway? Who says make-up is just for females? Do whatever makes you happy and don't worry about other people's opinions.

Olivia loves make-up but in my opinion she could go to an event without any on and still look completely stunning. Her skin is so fresh and you can see her freckles when she doesn't wear foundation. I love that. She doesn't need to wear make-up. To me she looks better without it than when she has on loads of it. I don't think that's a rude thing to say, she's just naturally so attractive she can get away with going bare-faced if she wants to.

I have nothing against women wearing as much make-up as they want, but when you see some girls up close and they've got so much foundation on it looks almost painful I don't like it. It's all very well looking good in pictures but when you see someone who looks like they've drawn on their face it's weird. Sixteen-year-old girls can easily look twenty-five these days, which scares me. Heavy make-up is not really my taste.

I was pretty low-maintenance when I was young. From the

age of fifteen until I was eighteen I used to cut my own hair. I'd sit down on the floor in front of the mirror in the bathroom and hold a hand-held mirror up so I could see the back of my head and I'd snip away. I always thought it looked okay but then when I was eighteen I went to a barbers to get my hair cut and I looked in the mirror afterwards and thought 'Oh my God, what have I been doing? Why has no one ever said anything about how shit my hair is?' Nowadays my hair is one of the most important things to me and if it's not right I don't feel right. Everything else can be on point but if your hair's not how you like it, everything else looks shit.

One of the best haircuts I've ever had was when Kem did it on *Love Island*. He did it again when we were shopping in Selfridges in London a few weeks after we'd left the villa. I'm not kidding, he just walked into a salon inside the shop and asked if he could use their equipment to cut my hair. And they let him! He washed it for me and everything, and forty-five minutes later I came out with a new look.

• • • • •

I had to slow things down in all areas of my life when I was sixteen because I got glandular fever. I'd had pleurisy, which is an inflammation of the tissues between your lungs and your chest, the year before and ended up in hospital, so I wasn't as healthy as I could have been. I also had quite a lot of other illnesses, like chickenpox and mumps, so I don't think I've got the strongest immune system generally.

The glandular fever came out of nowhere. I started to get tired a lot and I kept being sick. I also got breathless from doing the simplest things, which wasn't like me at all. Obviously I was massively sporty, so I couldn't understand why all of a sudden I was too tired to make it through an entire football match. The problem is you can't see an illness like glandular fever. The only physical sign is swollen glands, so I put it down to having a cold or being a bit run-down. I had no idea it was something more serious.

I was properly knocked out and after a while it became obvious it wasn't a short-lived virus. Eventually my mum took me to our local doctors. They did some blood tests for glandular fever and they came back positive. I was ill for a few months and I did get down at times. I was used to being really active but I had no choice but to take things easy for a while, and sleep a lot. Even now if I overdo things and get tired I get run-down really easily, and I think it's probably all to do with being so ill back then.

• • • • •

I didn't go to a lot of parties when I was in my teens because they weren't my thing. People used to ask me why I didn't go to things like there was something wrong with me, but they used to bore me. I much preferred playing sport. Girls did try to crack on to me sometimes but back then I was a bit oblivious to it. I wasn't the best when it came to girls generally.

When I was in Year 10 I got friendly with a girl called Bex, who was in my year. She was on me the whole time but nothing ever happened between us. It's weird that I didn't get with her because she's a really attractive girl and she was obsessed with me for a good couple of years. I'd go home from school every day and Bex would call my house phone and ask for me. I used to pretend to be out and she'd end up speaking to my dad instead. It happened every single night and I wasn't exactly subtle about blowing her off.

The funny thing is that Bex is one of my best mates now. I can literally talk to her about anything and I totally believe that men and women can just be friends. Sometimes I find it much easier to talk to a girl than I do a guy. Bex is really good with certain topics and I can be really open with her. It's always good to get her perspective on things.

I can talk to her about anything and I feel like she's the person I can be most open with. She knows me top to bottom and it's really nice to have a best friend who's a girl because they can give you a different perspective on things. I can talk to her if I'm feeling a bit down, and I've talked to her about relationship problems over the years. She's always really honest with me, which I massively appreciate.

I only started to give a shit about girls in anything beyond a friendship way when I was like sixteen and that's when I had my first girlfriend. She was called Emily and she went to the same school as me. We were together for about four or five months and we got on really well and she was a lovely girl. But then I realised that I wasn't really feeling it and so I decided to split up with her. It was the first time I'd ever broken up with anyone and it was not a good experience. I was only young so shamefully I did it over the phone, which is the worst thing you can do. She burst into hysterics and I didn't know what to do.

Would me going to talk to her help matters or make them worse? I felt terrible. No wonder I'd avoided relationships before that one. It definitely put me off for a while.

I dated a few girls here and there but I didn't really settle down with anyone. I didn't see the point in getting into something heavy. When I did meet girls I liked they didn't tend to be from around my way. I'd meet them through

Facebook or via mutual friends. I found it more exciting being with someone who lived a bit further away so no one knew them and people couldn't interfere.

Because I wasn't very switched on with girls I didn't end up losing my virginity until I was eighteen, which is considered pretty old. It didn't bother me that I was still a virgin while all my friends were having sex. My mates would talk about girls and I'd kind of switch off. It wasn't that I was shy, I just wasn't that interested in girls. Then all of a sudden I started to get a bit interested.

The first time I properly got with a girl was when my mate Josh and I were house-sitting for my cousin Stuart and his girlfriend Lexy and we invited a couple of girls over. We were trying to get their hot tub going but it wouldn't warm up and the cold water wasn't that enticing.

I still wasn't feeling a massive amount of pressure to lose my virginity, and I didn't have any idea we were going to end up having sex that night. We invited the girls round for a bit of fun and I basically lucked out. It honestly didn't feel like a big thing. We did it, she left and that was that. I had a shower and texted my mates, because that's what lads do, and then life went on as normal.

Having sex was pretty much what I was expecting and I didn't wake up feeling really manly the next day. I wouldn't say it was the best sexual experience of my life, and I think most people will say that about their first time. I suppose I was just pleased to get it out of the way.

The girl I slept with wasn't expecting anything from me and vice versa, so nothing happened afterwards. But I guess it got me into the swing of things and it was just before I started going away with my mates on holidays so at least there wasn't that worry that my first time might be with a total stranger I'd met in a bar five minutes before.

I went on my first lads' holiday to Magaluf when I was seventeen and it was heavy. There were nine of us and on the first night we went to a bar where we got given a sambuca shot each for free. No one else wanted theirs so I thought I'd be the big man and down them all. I wasn't used to drinking because I didn't drink that often back then. I'd mainly go for a few pints with my mates in the local pub on weekends and get a bit tipsy, but after those shots I got absolutely paralytic in ten minutes flat. It was a typical lads' holiday and I spent most of the time drinking fish bowls of cocktails and then being hungover.

I don't mind hangovers too much on holiday because you've usually got a pool, which seems to magically cure them, and you can also sweat them out or eat your way through them. I'm terrible with hangovers generally though. I really struggle. I hate being stuck inside feeling like shit. I moan a lot and make people really aware that I'm feeling shit.

I went on a few lads' holidays after that, to places like Malia in Crete and Rhodes, and I met a few girls here and there, but I've never put myself about. Even now I haven't slept with loads of people. I've only had sex with fourteen people, which isn't a massive number. I was in a committed relationship for a long time, and even before and after that I didn't ever feel the need to get my numbers up to impress other people. It's not a numbers game and I hate to think that lads or girls are sleeping around just so they can boast to their mates that they have.

One of my friends has got a list of women he's slept with on his phone. He can name every single one of them even though he doesn't remember who some of them are, and it's a bit of a badge of honour for him. I guess it means more to some people than others, but I would hate it if I'd slept with so many people I couldn't even remember them.

I've never cheated on anyone in my life. People are always really surprised when I say that but I think it's such a selfish thing to do. I don't get cheating. If you don't want to be with someone then split up with them, but don't go behind their back with someone else. If you feel like getting with someone new you obviously don't have the interest in your relationship that you should have. I couldn't live with myself if I cheated on someone. That's why it hurt so much when I was accused of cheating on Olivia, which we're going to come on to later in the book.

After that holiday my mates and I started getting more adventurous with going out. I think Magaluf gave us a bit of a taste for big nights out and Bournemouth was the closest place that had decent clubs, so we started going there most weekends.

I'd been a few times in the past and I'd got into clubs with fake ID. I used my mate's provisional driving licence and he was twenty-two at the time while I was seventeen, so I'm not sure how I got away with it.

We'd head down on a Friday night and stay in B&Bs and we'd end up spending most of the money we'd earned over the next couple of days. I remember the first time I went to a strip club there. I was so drunk I ended up spending every single penny I had in the bank, so I was totally broke. I'd had just shy of £1,000 in my account and when I woke up the following morning it was down to £0.

That's the problem with getting drunk, you lose sight of

what you should and shouldn't do and I was bad for that back then. I'm still not great at it sometimes these days to be fair.

• • • • •

My next relationship didn't happen until I was twenty and that one was my longest to date. And, before Olivia came along, it was my most serious one. It was with a girl called Victoria who lived in Northampton, which was about an hour from my home. Looking back I have no idea how we managed to keep a relationship going for so long. We used to have to alternate weekends at each other's house, but we made it work.

I met her through one of her best mates, who lived in Paxford, a village not far from my house. It was around Christmas time and we got introduced in a pub and hit it off. I thought she seemed like a nice girl and she was funny, and personality has always been massively important to me. You've got to get on well with each other if you're going to be spending a lot of time in each other's company.

We had a good relationship and we went on lots of trips and holidays together. We were together for three years in total, but to be honest from my point of view things started going a bit wrong after about two years. I kind of dragged it out for another six months to a year because I didn't know what else to do.

It was totally the wrong thing to do because I was falling out of love with her and the relationship had done its time. I guess I hoped the spark would somehow come back and it would all be okay again, but eventually I realised that wasn't going to happen. There was no one else involved and we still cared about each other a lot, but we couldn't go on the way we were.

It was heartbreaking when we split up but I knew it was what I needed to do. We were seeing each other less and less and she could tell I wasn't making as much effort as I had been. We had a really long chat over the phone one night and we both decided that it was best if we called it a day.

A lot of people knew us as a couple on Facebook, so rather than having to go round and tell everyone about the break-up individually we decided to put something on there letting people know instead. It felt like quite a strange thing to do but everything is done through social media now so no one batted an eyelid.

Victoria and I had a great few years together and she's still a mate of mine and she always will be, but not all relationships are supposed to last a lifetime. We went our separate ways with no hard feelings, which is the best way to end things.

Before I'd met Olivia I would have said Victoria was my first love, and in a way she was. But now I'm with Olivia I feel totally different because I've never loved anyone like I love her. I think if you love someone you want to be with them for ever. Victoria and I definitely loved each other but were we in love? In retrospect I'm not sure.

A story came out while I was on *Love Island* that I was still dating Victoria when I was in the villa. It was really weird because we'd split up a year previously, in the summer, and nothing had happened between us since. The press nicked some of her Instagram pictures and printed them, and they went through all her social media pages looking for anything interesting they could write about. They found a tweet she'd posted in 2015 where she said 'Desperation at its highest #loveisland.' So they reprinted it and made it into a bit of a story.

I spoke to her just after I left the show and she was pretty pissed off about it, understandably. We hadn't been together for months and months and she was now with someone else, and yet she was being dragged into my business and getting bombarded with messages from people she didn't know. She said that all she wanted to do was get on with her life and concentrate on work and all the drama had been really distracting. All I could suggest was for her to ignore it. I knew it would die down pretty quickly and there was nothing I could do about it in the meantime, but I did feel guilty about it. At the end of the day I'd made the decision to go on the show and she'd been dragged into it. Nothing bad or personal was written about her and it could have been a lot worse, but she could have done without it.

After Victoria and I broke up I did that typical post-split thing of going to the gym a lot. I started chatting to this girl called Hannah who always seemed to be in there at the same time as me. I made it quite clear I was interested but she was playing properly hard to get. Either that or she wasn't interested in me. I asked for her number and started texting her a bit, but I wasn't getting a lot of love back. I'd get a proper buzz when I saw her in the gym, but I don't think she felt the same.

Hannah was usually in the gym with her friend Charlotte, but one day Charlotte was in there on her own so we got chatting. When I got home that night I thought 'I actually think I quite like her too.' So I started messaging her as well. I was worried it might be a bit out of order but it wasn't like anything had happened, or looked like it was going to happen, between Hannah and me.

Charlotte and Hannah lived and worked together and one evening Hannah invited me round to watch the *Bake Off* final.

I'd never watched it in my life but I pretended I was really into it so I had an excuse to see the girls.

The three of us were drinking white wine and for some reason I was drinking it out of a pint glass. I'm not keen on wine, but it was all they had so I got stuck in. After a few of those I was so battered I barely knew where I was. I was so drunk I decided to stay over on the sofa and the girls both went to their bedrooms. At some point, and I'm not sure when or how, I ended up in Charlotte's bed and we slept together. I woke up at 6 a.m. the following day feeling terrible.

I was still properly boozed and I had to be in work at the solicitors at 9 a.m. It was horrific. Charlotte and I both looked at each other like 'What the hell has just happened?' Hannah came and knocked on the door and said, 'Is Chris in there?' and Charlotte replied, 'Yeah, he was really uncomfortable on the sofa so we top and tailed.' It was so awkward.

Hannah and Charlotte both went off to work and I stayed in bed thinking about the previous night. I called a taxi and got myself home and then somehow I managed to get myself ready and get to work. I spent the whole morning staring at my computer screen and then I said to someone 'I'm going to have to go home. I'm not okay here.' I went home and I slept for the rest of the day and still felt shit and really hungover when I woke up.

Charlotte and I started messaging each other a lot and I started staying over more. I thought it would be awkward with Hannah but actually it was fine. Let's face it; she clearly wasn't heartbroken because she was never actually into me.

The good thing about Charlotte is that she was quite like me in that she was happy to just chill out and watch films and eat nice food when we saw each other. She didn't always want to go out for expensive meals or go partying. To me that's what a nice date is. Just staying in and chatting and relaxing. I know people call it Netflix and Chill these days, but I honestly didn't know what Netflix was until a few months ago. I thought it was a word someone had made up. For some reason it totally passed me by. I guess I used to 'film and chill' instead.

I started to really like Charlotte and we had a lot of fun together, but then out of nowhere she started treating me like a bit of an idiot and expecting me to do everything for her. We were really off and on and we'd sack it off and not talk for a week, and then we'd end up meeting up again. It was really weird. When things were good they were great, but when things were shit they were really shit. It felt like she was treating our relationship as if it was a bit of a game and messing me about a lot, and I never knew where I was.

I was confused because I'd started to really like her, but when you get pushed away so many times I think you just stop caring. There are only so many times you can try to make something work when someone isn't treating you very well.

We both agreed we should split up around Christmas, the year before I went into *Love Island*. About three weeks later I was sat in a bar after playing golf and I got a WhatsApp message from Charlotte that was – and I'm not kidding – about sixty lines long. She said she missed me and she would do anything to get me back. She admitted she took me for granted and thought I'd always be there. I looked at the message and I didn't feel anything. I wasn't seeing anyone else at the time, but when you know you would rather be on your own than with someone it's not a great sign. I didn't know what to say so I ignored the message and I didn't ever hear from her again. She was the last person I was involved with before I went on the show, and I guess it was good that I was single for a while in the run-up.

I'm pretty confident in relationships on the whole. I get more excited than nervous when I'm with someone and that's how it should be. If you're worrying about things you're probably not with the right person. If it's meant to be it's meant to be, and if it's not you'll soon know about it.

I haven't been on many proper dates. You know, like when you ask someone out and then take them somewhere to impress them? That hasn't really happened a lot. I've only been out with a few people and they've turned into relationships straight away so I haven't done the whole impressing them with big gestures thing.

I've never, ever been out with someone I've met on Tinder or any of the other apps either. I did sign up to Tinder once but I fucking hated it. I only did it for banter and because my mates were on there too. Online and app dating does seem to work really well for some people but I find it weird that you're just basing whether or not you like someone on a picture. You're judging them on that alone and they might be really good-looking but a really awful person.

Also, so many people catfish on those sites. Someone once set up a profile calling themselves 'Craig' using all my pictures. They must have nicked them from somewhere and then they pretended to be me. The same thing happened after the show. Several people have set up social media accounts in my name and messaged girls making out they were me and all sorts. One person who did that ended up causing me no end of bother, but we'll come on to that later.

Some of my mates have been catfished in the past. They've

turned up to meet a girl and they've looked nothing like their Tinder pictures. My friends have pretended to go to the loo and then done a runner but I couldn't do that. I couldn't be that harsh. I would feel so bad. I'd have to be honest with them even though I hate awkward situations. Knowing me I'd probably end up staying for a drink even if they were a million miles away from my type.

To be fair, though, if you do catfish you kind of deserve to be walked out on. You should always be honest on dating apps because you're going to get found out eventually.

It's a shame people don't feel like they can be themselves. That makes me sad. There is someone for everyone out there and not everyone looks like a supermodel. We're all good enough in our own way, flaws and all.

I'm definitely not anti-apps or websites because so many people have got together with people and got married and all sorts, but it's just not for me. Even if I did give it a go I would know within two minutes of talking or messaging someone if I wanted to meet up with them or not. I'm not saying I'm the least shallow person in the world because I'm really not, and of course you've got to fancy someone to go out with them. But I honestly couldn't date a girl, no matter how good-looking she was, if she didn't have any banter. I couldn't be with someone who had nothing going on upstairs.

I don't reckon I could ever go on a dating app now. It would be well weird. People would probably think my account was fake. I'm not that bothered about not being in a relationship. I'm quite happy working and being me for me for a while.

I'm not one of those people who has to be in a relationship

all the time to be happy. If I hadn't met Olivia in the villa I would have come out of there as a single bloke and my first thought would *not* have been girls.

The last time I . . .

Laughed so much it hurt

When I was with a load of my old mates and we were bantering.

Got annoyed

When I was driving on a motorway and someone flashed me for no reason.

Fibbed

My mum asked me if I was all right and I said I was even though I was bare stressed.

Wore something dodgy

I bought a blue, white and black Adidas tracksuit that I think is well nice but other people hate it, so probably that.

Was embarrassed

I don't get embarrassed. I don't think I've got any shame.

Used public transport

Is a tube public transport? I used one about two weeks ago to get from one side of London to the other.

Got told off by my mum

When I was staying back home and I told her I needed a specific T-shirt washed half an hour before I was leaving. She got annoyed and said I should have given her more notice.

Spent loads of money

I went out with my friends in Soho and spent over a grand on drinks and taxis. It was a good night though.

Felt properly relaxed

When I had a massage at a spa recently.

Surprised

Every time something that isn't true is written about me.

Cut someone's call

It was my friend Josh. I called him a twat and put the phone down on him but it was only a joke.

3

Fight Club

After I finished at school I wanted to stay on for the sixth form and do A-level PE. At first they wouldn't let me because of my terrible theory score, but in the end, after a lot of talking them round, they changed their minds and let me on the course. In the end though I only lasted a week anyway.

I chose to study science alongside PE because we had to choose another subject to study, and I didn't enjoy that at all. I knew pretty much straight away that I wasn't going to stick it out. I was literally only interested in sport and it was a real chore having to go to lectures about chemistry and try to remember stuff.

I wanted to concentrate on sport full time, so after I dropped out of sixth form I got a place at Hartpury College and did a National Diploma in Football, Sport and Excellence. The standard of football was unbelievable and I instantly knew I'd made the right choice. The rugby talent there is also so strong it's on a par with Loughborough College, which is famous for being amazing sports-wise.

I had been playing football since I was twelve at the Swindon Centre of Excellence, which is basically a training academy. I played in the Milk Cup, which is a world-renowned competition in Northern Ireland that teams from all around the world take part in. Our youth team beat Watford in the finals to win one year, and people like David Beckham have also played in that cup so it was a big achievement.

I was released from Swindon when I was sixteen and after that I went to play for Cheltenham for three months. I had trials and nearly signed a deal with them, but it didn't happen in the end. That's when I decided Hartpury would be my next step.

• • • • •

I would honestly say the Hartpury Academy team is as good as some professional youth teams. It was like the Manchester United of football colleges. We won the National Colleges competition two years running, and we got treated like we were fully qualified while we were there. I was thinking seriously about a long-term career in football at that point and it suited me much better than sitting in a classroom learning about the periodic table.

I trained three or four times a week and Wednesday was always our big game day. I'd do sporting assignments too so it wasn't all about playing, and there was an academic side to it. You had to put the work in and prove that you deserved your place. They really brought out the best in me and I think some of my best footballing years happened while I was there.

We had a manager called Steve Gwynne, who is an ex pro

footballer, so he was incredibly knowledgeable and really pushed us. If you weren't up to standard he'd make sure you knew about it. I'm the kind of person who only concentrates on what they enjoy so it suited me so much better than learning about the periodic table.

I travelled to the academy every day for the first year I was there, and then in my second year I stayed in halls, which was the first time I'd lived away from home. It was strange standing on my own two feet for the first time ever, but for some reason I didn't feel nervous about it. I was more nervous about passing my course than anything else.

One of my best mates, Jay, stayed on the campus as well, so it was a good laugh. I felt much more involved in my course when I lived there. I didn't go to university but I got a taste of what it would have been like during that time.

Our block shared a kitchen and I had to cook food for myself quite a lot. Well, I say cook, I mainly had ready meals, or Jay and I would get takeaways or go out to eat. My mum used to give me a bit of money every week. I think she was worried I wouldn't eat properly otherwise.

I went home most weekends and a lot of my mates did the same. It was boring there if no one was around. I always took my washing back for my mum to do, and it was nice catching up with my family and my mates.

I wouldn't say I grew up massively around that time because I was still being looked after a lot, but it was the beginning of me getting more independence and not relying on my parents quite as much.

It was while I was in the second year of Hartpury that I first started going on proper nights out. There aren't many bars and clubs around where I grew up, but Hartpury is really near Cheltenham and Gloucester, both of which are pretty decent for going out. Especially in comparison to where I'm from.

We had a bit of a routine and on Mondays we'd go into Cheltenham and on Wednesdays we'd go to Gloucester. It was always safe to go out on a Monday because we didn't ever have matches on a Tuesday. But we didn't ever go out on a Tuesday because there's nothing worse than trying to play a game when you're feeling shit. Plus, Steve would have gone mad if he'd found out we were hungover. Our going out was monitored and we never pushed our luck.

Sometimes we wouldn't decide to go out until 11 o'clock at night and even if I wasn't in the mood for it my mates would manage to convince me to go. We'd either get a taxi into town or jump on a bus, and we'd head to places we knew served cheap drinks. I didn't do the crazy student thing of drinking every night or getting so drunk I didn't remember what I'd done.

It was rare for me to go totally over the top because to be fair I didn't really have the money to, but I remember one night my mate Jay and I got really smashed. We got a taxi back to our halls but when we got there we realised we didn't have any money. To make things worse Jay had been sick in the back of the cab so the driver was well annoyed and wanted to charge us loads extra.

We didn't want to be arseholes and do a runner, so in the end Jay went upstairs to his room and got his X-Box and used that as payment. We were so gutted when we woke up the next day and realised what he'd done. It was worth a bloody fortune.

I'll be honest: I always did all right with girls on our nights out and I didn't have a lot of worries about pulling; I'd dart around taking my pick thinking I was the dog's bollocks. I may have been a late developer when it came to girls, but that didn't affect my confidence.

I'm not the kind of guy to go round a bar chatting girls up. I was always in decent shape and I think being sporty helps with the women. I usually just look at them and flutter my eyelashes and hope they don't think I'm being weird. I can't wink because I've got a bone missing around my eye, which is something I was born with, so if I try I end up blinking instead. I think it's a bit of a blessing because winking at someone can look a bit creepy. In a way I think nature has done me a favour not giving me that ability.

I used to drink vodka or gin and lemonade a bit back then but I hated whisky. I was never one of those people who was stumbling around clubs hammered, and I was never sick or anything. I felt like I was in control of myself most of the time, and even if I drank a lot I was never slumped against walls about to pass out or getting involved in fights. I had mates who would go out looking for fights but I never got it. I'd see guys staring each other out in clubs and you could sense that a scrap was about to break out.

When I got a bit older, around nineteen or twenty, it was almost like a given that something would kick off every time I went out with my mates. It would never be about anything in particular but I always knew when it was coming. I didn't ever start fights, and I was never one to pile in. I preferred watching from the sidelines.

One of my mates got bottled in a fight and he split his eyebrow open. He was so drunk he went home and went to sleep and it wasn't until the next morning he looked in the

Me as a baby with my dad. I don't know why he's got his finger in my mouth?

This is my brother Ben giving me a kiss. He wasn't always that nice to me.

I'm with my brother Will in this one. I look well peaceful. That didn't last long.

Looking innocent in my christening dress. Little did my
parents know I was going to cry all day.

Ben and me with my mum and dad. My parents have still got those curtains.

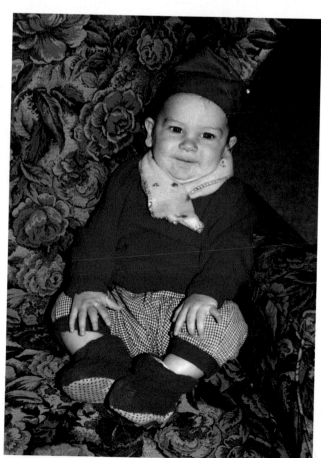

My mum made this Noddy outfit for me. The scarf is actually a duster. It's well clever.

This is me, my dad and our dog Eley hanging out at my granddad's farm when I was around three. Check out my Barbour and flat cap.

This is me with all my brothers. I've got no idea whose birthday it was but the cake looks very nice.

I bloody loved Thomas the Tank Engine. I wish I still had that shirt. I reckon Ben's pulling that face because he's jealous of it.

This was taken in Bournemouth on the same day I threw sand in my dad's face. He was not happy.

This was one of my favourite dressing up outfits. Look
at those amazing trousers.

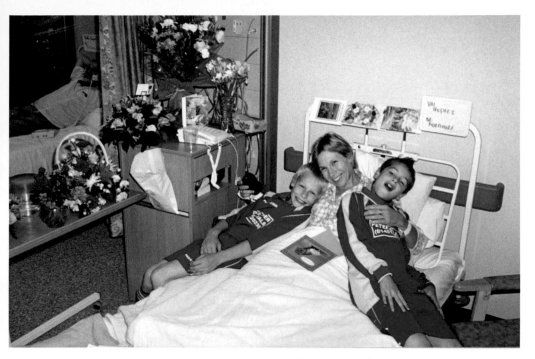

Ben and I visited my mum in hospital after she had her heart attack. We're smiling but it was such an awful time.

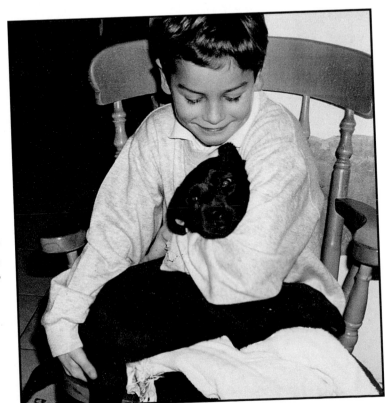

This is me with my dog Rowan. Do you think he looks like he's desperate to get away?

Getting in training for Love Island when I was about 11. Nice tan.

If you haven't got a horse handy a giant Tigger
and a knitting needle will do.

mirror and thought 'Shit' and got himself down to the hospital. I think fighting is something blokes grow out of and I've only ever had one fight in my entire life. It was with my best mate Jay, the same guy I went to Hartpury with, and it's so weird thinking back to it because his mum and dad are like my second parents and he's been so good to me since I left *Love Island*. We had a proper fist-fight and it's the first and only time I've thrown a punch.

It happened when I was giving him and my other mate Max a lift into town on a night out. We were eighteen and I'd passed my driving test first time when I was seventeen, so I was driving the first ever car I had, which was a Golf my dad had kindly bought me. Jay had been drinking and all of a sudden he was sick in my car. I had a go at him and he started giving me loads of abuse, and I lost my shit, so we had a big row. I was doing him a favour giving him a lift and he was being stroppy with me even though he was the one who'd made a right mess of my car.

We stopped in the middle of a housing estate so he could get out and get some air and we started arguing again. My car window was open and Jay walked over and punched me through it. I got out of the car and we squared up to each other and then started having a full-on fight.

Max jumped out of the car and tried to break it up, but he was in the wrong place at the wrong time because when I went to hit Jay I ended up punching Max instead. We were making a lot of noise and this woman ran out of her house and said she was going to call the police. Max and I got back in the car and drove off and when the police arrived they ended up taking Jay home and giving him a bollocking.

Jay messaged me the next day saying sorry and that he was

going to make it up to me. We were due to go and see Chelsea and Sunderland play the following weekend and he said he was going to pay for the whole thing and drive us both there, so I forgave him straight away. If you're good enough mates with someone you can piss each other off and get away with it. And you do stupid things when you're young, don't you?

To me a good friend is someone you can fall out with and always know it's going to be okay in the end. A proper mate is also someone you can tell something to, safe in the knowledge that they're going to keep it to themselves. If someone can keep a secret you know they're a good person. Friends look out for each other and they listen to each other and they keep things to themselves.

I've had the same friends for years, whether they're from football, cricket, school or riding. I know I can trust every single one of them and they've got my back. The people who are with you from the beginning are the ones who will be with you until the end (deep).

· · · · ·

After I left Hartpury I did think about going to uni for a while but it just wasn't for me. I applied to five different places and I got offered some interviews, but in the end I sacked it off. Instead I ended up going to Kettering for three months to play football for Kettering Town.

I stayed in Travelodges during the week and went home at weekends. So I could get my washing done and get some decent food, obviously. It was a good experience and I met some really nice people, but the club was all over the place. It was a shame because they'd signed some big footballers who had just been released from pro teams and we had a decent squad, but the money was so bad I couldn't afford to stay there in the end.

They offered me a weekly wage but I had to pay rent and live off it and I was always broke. Even though I was doing something I loved it wasn't enough to keep me going and I wanted to start earning decent money.

I was already thinking about leaving the club, and then one weekend when I was back home my decision was made for me. I was messing about on my bed and I jumped off and somehow landed on the wrong foot. My knee jarred and I screamed my head off.

Ben was the only other person in the house at the time and I was in so much agony I hobbled from my room to the landing to try to get his attention. I was so angry I punched a picture that was hanging on the wall and all the glass smashed. I was in a horrible amount of pain and on top of that I cut my knuckle too, which didn't help matters.

I shouted to Ben to get me a phone so I could ring my mum or an ambulance. He said I was being dramatic and that I'd probably just twisted my knee and it would eventually click back into place. I wanted to kill him, and I was so angry I picked up a bit of the broken glass and chucked it at him. What a dick! Thankfully it missed him but he was so pissed off with me he went out and left me on my own. It took me two hours to drag myself down the stairs to the phone. The tiniest movement was painful, so I could only move about an inch at a time.

I rang my mum and I ended up going to hospital the same day. They did an X-ray and then put a brace on my leg. I had torn some ligaments and I'd ripped all the cartilage and it was wedged at the side of my knee. I was told I'd need an operation and a few months later I ended up having keyhole surgery. Although it helped long-term, the pain at the time was unbelievable. I couldn't sleep properly because every time I turned over the pain in my knee would wake me up. It was a difficult time.

· · · · ·

It took around six months for my knee to get better, and I knew there was no way I could go back to playing football as a job. It was clear that I would never be able to play like I had before. My knee hasn't been the same since and even now it still causes me pain. I turned to get the ball during a match with some mates a while back and as I did I felt my knee go. It swelled up so badly I had to stop playing and leave the pitch.

Luckily I think I'd had my fill of football by that time so it didn't bother me too much. I'd fallen out of love with playing, and looking back I'd probably felt that way for a while. I'd been given a lot of great opportunities and my parents had been really supportive, but it was time to do something new.

I will always love football and I really enjoy going to watch it. I became a Sunderland supporter at a young age because of my Uncle Alan. He wasn't actually my uncle, he was a close family friend, but that's what I always called him.

Sadly he died a while back but he used to live in Sunderland. From when I was three years old he used to send me the *Sunderland Echo* every week. Once I could read I used to love it, and I always liked looking at the football pages. As a result I became a Sunderland fan.

I went to my first game in 2000 in Leeds and that was it.

After that I'd go two or three times a season and I went to see Sunderland playing Man U several times. I'm not sure why I used to go and see them because we always got spanked and barely touched the ball.

I still get to play football every now and again these days. I played in a charity football match for the Bradley Lowery Foundation at Goodison Park in Liverpool last September, alongside some ex-pros and people like Olly Murs and Shayne Ward.

I had a personal appearance booked in that day but I cancelled it straight away because the game was so much more important.

Bradley affected people in such an amazing way. Even though he was incredibly ill with neuroblastoma, a rare form of cancer, and had been since he was just eighteen months old, he was always so positive and happy. Tragically he died last July at the age of six. He was a warrior and it felt great to be a part of such an amazing day. It was a real honour.

I've got to go to some incredible sporting events since *Love Island*. I got the opportunity to play in the Masters Pro-Am golf tournament at Close House in Newcastle. I played with Ian Poulter, who is one of the best golfers in the world, and he's such a brilliant person.

I also went to ex-England international cricketer Ryan Sidebottom's testimonial up in Yorkshire. I played a match with Liam Plunkett and Gary Ballance, who are England pros. I made some really good new friends that day. I've been so fortunate.

• • • • •

I was a happy kid throughout my teens and I didn't ever suffer from any kind of self-esteem, anxiety or mental health issues.

I remember being down around the time I had glandular fever, but I think that was more frustration that I couldn't do all the things I wanted to. Other than that I was always pretty together and stress-free. Then suddenly when I was nineteen that all changed.

One night when I was lying in bed after a night out this weird feeling came over me. For some reason my whole body started to feel empty and it was horrendous. I can't really explain it but it was like I felt hollow and fragile. I had a real sense of fear about everything. It wasn't anything specific; it was like an underlying panic that something bad was going to happen, but I didn't know what.

The following day I felt the same and even speaking to my family felt a little bit overwhelming. I'd never experienced anything like that in my life and it was so confusing. I thought maybe I was coming down with glandular fever again because it would explain why I was feeling low, but physically I felt fine. It was just my head that was doing weird stuff. I felt like I'd lost control over it.

Things didn't improve over the following few days and in the end I felt like I had no choice but to speak to my mum about it. She suggested I went to see my doctor, but I felt embarrassed and like I should be able to deal with it on my own. There wasn't any kind of pattern to it and it was hard to keep track of. It would happen randomly so there weren't any particular triggers, which meant I was always on edge in case it suddenly came on.

I kept it really well hidden from everyone apart from my mum at that point, but she could see I wasn't getting any better and eventually she said to me, 'This has gone on too long and you need to get it sorted.'

In the end I agreed to see the doctor. He gave me the chance to explain everything and then he said really calmly, 'What you're describing there is anxiety.' Obviously I knew something was wrong with me but I was still quite taken aback because I'd never experienced anything like that before.

I really didn't want to take any tablets and I hoped it would get better on its own. It had come on so quickly I kept praying it would disappear just as fast. No such luck.

I was working full time in the solicitors' office by then and I carried on as normal, going to work every day and keeping my mind occupied. I enjoyed it even though it wasn't my dream job. Plus the money was good and it kept me busy. That was one of the most important things for me. I needed that focus. I soon realised that keeping myself active was a really good way to literally take my mind off how I was feeling.

Every day at work when it got to around 4.30 p.m. I'd start seriously clock-watching. Not because I was desperate to leave, but because I knew that once I walked out the door I wouldn't have anything to occupy my mind and the anxiety would kick in. As soon as I got in the car and I had space to think, the feelings of panic would take over and my busy mind would start kicking off again. I didn't even know the root cause but when I looked at my life, on the surface I didn't actually have any worries.

I was constantly anxious about being anxious. So I was stuck in a catch 22 situation where if I wasn't feeling anxious I would worry about it anyway. I was always preparing myself for the worst. I got myself in a cycle and I couldn't get away from it. It's the scariest thing I've ever been through.

I kept beating myself up because no matter what I did, whether it was keeping busy or exercising, nothing would help. The anxiety always seemed to be winning. I'd get a thought in my head and it would whirr round and round for hours. The stupid thing was I didn't have any real worries that I could put my finger on. It wasn't like I knew there was a root cause that I could try to deal with by having some counselling.

Looking back I wonder whether it could have been triggered by some of the things that happened earlier in my teenage years. Maybe I didn't properly deal with stressful situations, like my mum's heart attack, and so they crept back up on me. I'd always thought of myself as happy-go-lucky and this new anxious Chris just wasn't me.

I tried to keep myself occupied every weekend and I'd make sure I had loads of things to do so I could distract myself as much as possible. I was around my mates a lot but I didn't ever speak to them about it. I felt ashamed, but that was the anxiety playing tricks on me. I was worried people would judge me or think I was weak for having those feelings.

I would go to bed every night feeling terrified because I was on my own with too much time to think. I found it really hard to get to sleep because my mind was all over the shop and I felt like my thoughts were suffocating me, and even when I had got to sleep I'd sometimes wake up in a state of panic. I used to go to the toilet a lot in the middle of the night when I didn't need to just so I had a distraction and a few minutes' respite from my manic head. I needed to do something – anything – to stop the thoughts.

Our local gym was open late so often I'd go in there at around 10 p.m. hoping to wear myself out enough so I could sleep for a few hours at least. I also went through a phase of taking my car out at three or four in the morning because when I had to concentrate on driving my head was a bit calmer.

Sport was definitely a massive outlet for me when I was suffering from the anxiety. Any footballer will tell you that no matter what worries you've got, once you're on a football pitch you forget everything. All your worries fall by the wayside and the sport takes over. It gives you something to focus on and look forward to, and I did a lot of fitness stuff when I wanted to distract my busy mind. It was a release for me and I could let off a lot of steam. But really all the things I did were just temporary distractions.

Even though doing certain activities provided me with a bit of respite, no matter what I did I couldn't shake off the feelings of doom. After a few months of not sleeping and feeling constantly on edge I was mentally and physically exhausted. There were times when I honestly wondered if I was going mad.

I remember sitting up in bed one night praying my head would calm down long enough for me to go to sleep. That was the point when I started to understand why people who suffer from depression kill themselves. That was my lowest point because even though I wasn't suicidal, I was reasoning with the concept of it, and that was incredibly scary. The fact that I was even thinking along those lines and feeling an affinity with people who take their own lives was horrendous.

It's hard because people who don't suffer from anxiety or depression don't really get it, I guess. It's hard to put yourself in the shoes of someone who is going through such a shitty time that they don't even want to live any more. But in that moment I got it. Like I said, I didn't ever think 'I want to kill myself', but my anxiety was so bad I could understand why some people craved a way to escape.

I finally reached breaking point one evening after I left work. It felt like someone was screaming inside my head and I didn't know what to do to shut them up. When I got home I spoke to Mum and I was completely honest about everything I was feeling. I'd tried to pretend to everyone around me that I was feeling better but there was no hiding it any more.

It was such a massive relief to tell someone. From that point on I didn't feel like I was dealing with it on my own any more. At last I was being honest with myself about the fact I couldn't win this fight on my own.

Over the next week or so I also spoke to my dad and my brothers about what had been going on, and they were nothing but supportive and encouraging. I felt like a giant weight had been lifted knowing I had a lot of support around me.

It was like I'd taken the first step towards getting better. The second one was getting professional help. I went and saw a hypnotherapist called David Crees in Cheltenham, and he used this weird but effective method where I had to turn my dark thoughts into shapes. I had to imagine my bad thoughts as triangles and my good thoughts as circles, and I'd try to turn the triangles into circles. It sounds mad but it bloody worked.

He also taught me breathing techniques where I had to breathe in and out really slowly so I could break down the adrenalin that kicked in inside my body whenever I was anxious. It wasn't an overnight cure but I learnt some brilliant techniques that helped me to cope better with it moving forward.

Slowly but surely the feelings of panic started to slip away and my sleep improved. It helped so much to speak to someone who was outside of my family and friends circle because I was completely uncensored, and I knew that everything I told him would stay between us. I could be totally honest with him and know that whatever I said to him it wouldn't go any further.

Now when I get those same feelings, which still happens at times, I know how to deal with them. The fact that I've already overcome serious anxiety once means I know I can do it again.

If I hadn't spoken out and talked to my mum when I did I could have carried on suffering for months, or even years. And that's why I would always encourage people to share how they're feeling. It worked for me, and I honestly don't know what would have happened if I hadn't found the courage to talk to my family.

I wish I'd talked to them earlier because what I was going through didn't have a negative effect on any of my relationships. If anything it brought me closer to people. Everyone's reactions were brilliant and all they wanted to do was help me. I'd never really opened up to my dad about stuff like that before but he was amazing and so supportive.

Honestly, I would say to anyone who is going through similar stuff please don't be scared to be open. That's the first step in getting help and getting over difficult times.

My FAVOURite Stuff

Book
The Twits by Roald Dahl. I read it when I was young and I still love it.

Film
I've got three – *Pretty Woman, Dumb and Dumber* and *Shooter* with Mark Wahlberg. And the original *Point Break*. I've got four.

Saying
'That's banter, surely?'

Outfit
I like proper matching tracksuits like Adidas or Nike.

Song
'Matchbox' by The Kooks.

Band
The View and The Kooks.

Memory
When a horse called Synchronised won the 2012 Gold Cup.
It was trained by Jonjo O'Neill, who is a good family friend.
The finish of the race was unbelievable.

Celeb lady
Jessica Alba is my celeb crush.

Animal
Cows.

Possession
My Rolex watch. I got it from Hatton Garden.

4

Oh Balls

After waving farewell to my footballing career I decided it was about time I started earning some decent money for once. That's when I got a full-time job working for my cousin Jamie's solicitors firm doing conveyancing, which is basically dealing with all the legal stuff that's involved when people buy and sell houses.

To become a licensed conveyancer I had to do a lot of training and get qualifications, but once I'd done that it was all about sticking to a formula so it was pretty straightforward. It's a lot of work but once you've got the hang of it you're away.

The company was based in a town called Chipping Campden quite near where I lived, so it was local but I still had to get myself up early every day and get there on time, which has always been a bit of a struggle for me. I suppose that was the first time I had proper responsibilities so I couldn't get away with being slack. I was earning regular money. And sadly spending it way too regularly.

I'd only ever lived on my own when I was at Hartpury College, and when I turned twenty I decided it was time to take a big leap and move out of my parents' house. I was a bit split because on the one hand I loved living at home, but on the other I needed to have some more independence. A lot of my mates were away at uni or they were living on their own, and I couldn't rely on my mum to look after me for ever.

I rented a house that was on its own in the middle of a field, so to be fair it wasn't like I moved to a big city and started a completely new life. The new place was only ten minutes up the road from my family home so I could pop home and get a proper cooked meal or some logs for the fire (I love an open fire) any time I wanted. But I felt like I had to try to experience what it was like to do everything for myself. As it turns out, I was useless.

I was rubbish at paying the rent on time and the place was always a bit of a mess. I lived by myself and it was weird being on my own after having people around me for so long. It may sound a bit wimpy but I found it scary at times because there weren't any other houses within walking distance if anything dramatic happened. Mind you, I wasn't on my own for long. After a while my mate Josh tended to stay on the sofa most nights so it ended up being his pit as well. You can imagine what a state it was then.

• • • • •

One night in the middle of winter Josh and I went back to my parents' farm quite late at night to collect some logs. As we went down the drive I noticed that the swing gates to one of the barns had been left open. It was strange because my dad or Ben would always make sure all the doors were securely locked before they left at night, and leaving one open wasn't something they would have done by mistake. They were always really careful about that kind of thing.

We parked up and Josh walked over and looked inside the barn and said to me, 'Where's the tractor?' I rang my dad and Ben straight away and both of them said it had been there when they'd left earlier that evening. The only explanation was that someone had stolen it. It must have been planned because nicking a tractor isn't something you suddenly decide to do. Decent tractors can be worth a couple of hundred grand so it's big business.

My dad phoned the police and they immediately drove around the area trying to track it down. I had a good idea of who might have stolen it because they'd nicked some other stuff from us previously, so Josh and I drove in the direction of where they live in case we came across it. Quite often tractors are put on a container and shipped to another area within hours of being stolen, so we didn't hold out much hope.

Some friends of the family were also keeping an eye out for us and one of them spotted it parked in the middle of a field near a quiet country lane. The police soon confirmed it was ours and it was returned to us, but it was all a bit of a drama.

As I mentioned, that wasn't the first time we'd been burgled. In 2014 ten of the huge, heavy batteries that are used to power our electric fences were nicked. They can be worth a lot of money if they're scrapped so someone obviously knew they were there and spotted an opportunity to make some quick cash.

When Dad checked all the buildings to see if anything else was missing he noticed that the quad bike key wasn't in its usual place. The quad bike was still parked where it always was but the key had definitely been swiped.

Dad phoned the police and they said that if the key was missing, the likelihood was the thieves would be back the following day to steal the bike too. Their theory was that the thieves had planned to just nick the batteries, but as they were leaving they spotted the valuable quad bike but had no way to transport it off the land. The police reckoned they were going to source a trailer and come back when it was dark so they could steal it.

That night two female police officers came to the farm to do a bit of a stakeout. An emergency call came in so one of the officers had to take the car and head to Stow-on-the-Wold, which is the next town along from us. The other police officer stayed with Dad and me. We heard a car coming down the drive about an hour later and we assumed it was her colleague coming back.

The road up to the farm is unlit so it's very dark, meaning you can't see who anyone is until they enter the driveway. We were all poised to see a police car pulling up but instead a green Golf started driving really slowly into the barn area.

They spotted us and the car did the quickest three-point turn I've ever seen. The police officer stood in front of the car to try to get them to stop, but instead of slowing down they sped up and knocked her over. Then they raced back up the drive as fast as they could.

Amazingly the officer wasn't hurt and somehow in the midst of everything she managed to get the registration number of the car. She phoned it in straight away and the police sent out a squad car to try to find them. Dad and I jumped into his Land Rover to try to chase them but they were well ahead of us and their car had kicked up so much dust we could barely see in front of us.

The police tracked down the car and when they questioned the owners these two lads held their hands up and admitted to the theft straight away. That was three years ago now and we haven't had any problems since, thankfully, but my dad is always on the lookout for any signs of people sniffing around. There is so much money sitting on farms, whether it's machinery or diesel, so they'll always be a prime target.

• • • • •

I didn't live away from home for very long. It was good to get out and spread my wings but I soon realised that life was much easier at home and I missed clean sheets magically appearing on my bed and piles of ironed clothes turning up in my room. It was also a lot cheaper and, as I've said, I wasn't the best at budgeting.

I didn't actually end up moving out of home properly until I moved in with Olivia after we came out of *Love Island*. I had it so good at home I didn't see any need to. I'd tried it and I didn't like it. I know twenty-four is quite old to still be living with your parents, but I get on really well with them so I didn't see anything wrong with it.

I enjoyed living at home. It's easy and you get proper home comforts. You don't have to worry about heating bills or things going wrong. My parents didn't expect me to pay rent even though I had a job. I was very fortunate. I still enjoy going back there now and it's my sanctuary in a way.

I'm not sure how my parents felt about me moving back in but at least my teenage strops had calmed. I was probably hard work until I got into my late teens. My parents don't take any shit and my dad would always tell me when I was being a nightmare. I used to sulk a lot and, no word of a lie, I still do now. I'll properly go in to one and I have to have a word with myself. See, I really haven't grown up.

I used to get really hangry if I hadn't eaten and my mum knew if I was kicking off, it meant that I had to eat something as soon as possible. Olivia and I had an argument at my parents' house one day about something really pointless. My mum knew I was being an arsehole so she said to Olivia, 'Sorry about this. He does it when he's hungry. He just needs to eat.' I'm bad when I'm hungry, I don't function well, but as soon as I eat I'm a nicer person. So if you ever see me in a bad mood, give me a sandwich.

• • • • •

I haven't been the luckiest with my health over the years, and from twenty-two onwards I ended up having four operations on my bollocks. Sorry, on my testicles. I was having a bath one day, and of course when you have a bath everything relaxes so you can see lumps and bumps more easily. That's when I spotted this large growth on my testicle.

I'd first noticed it when I was about fourteen and I remember thinking it looked like a really small cartoon brain. It was just a cluster of veins so I didn't pay much attention to it. I thought it would probably go away on its own eventually. Fourteen is a tricky age and I was too embarrassed to mention it to anyone. All sorts of things happen to your body when you're a teenager so I thought it was probably pretty standard and happened to a lot of boys.

That day in the bath, eight years later, I noticed that not

only was it still there, it had grown quite a lot, and it hit me that it could be something serious. I'd pushed it to the back of my mind but there was no denying it looked pretty horrible and would need some kind of medical attention. I spoke to my mum about it and then went to the doctor, and he was so calm about it I felt stupid for putting it off for so long.

It turned out I had a varicocele on my left testicle, which is a build-up of veins. I also had a hydrocele on my right testicle, which is a little sac filled with fluid. I also had some scans and they tested me for testicular cancer and I had an ultrasound and everything, which was terrifying. Thankfully they came back clear and it was such a relief to know I didn't have cancer.

Testicular cancer is something that's in my family so it was a real worry, but when I got the news that I was okay it made the varicocele and the hydrocele much easier to deal with. They felt like nothing compared to the possibility of having cancer. Neither were really serious but both needed treatment as soon as possible.

The main issue with a varicosity is that the veins take oxygen from the testicles, so the danger is if it's left untreated it could make you infertile.

As a result, I've had my sperm frozen because there was also a risk that my sperm would be affected by the treatments I had to have later on.

The hospital insisted on it, but it was something I wanted to do anyway so I didn't think twice. I was only twenty-two and they were effectively telling me it could be the only way for me to have a family in the future. There was no way I was going to refuse. They said it was only precautionary but it still played on my mind a lot because they were clearly concerned I might have a problem further down the line.

There's a history of infertility problems in my family so it was a big worry. If I couldn't have a family in the future it would be tragic. It's the one thing I want in life and I would really struggle to accept it if I couldn't have kids.

My sperm was frozen just before I had my first operation. When they did a count of the sample it was just below average. That's good because it means my count isn't *really* low, but it's still millions of sperm fewer than it could be. It's so clever that they have the technology to know how powerful my sperm is.

I had to go to Gloucester Hospital to give the sample. My dad came with me and it was weird because we both knew what I was there for but we didn't really talk about it. What was he going to say? 'How do you feel about your sperm being frozen, Chris?' I think we probably talked about everything *but* sperm.

I had to go into a room (on my own!) and do the deed. And no, there weren't any specialist magazines in there, and I didn't take my phone in with me so I could watch porn. That's probably why it took me a while to get the job done. I was in this little room for ages thinking 'My dad knows exactly what I'm doing in here. I wish I could hurry up.' But the more I thought about how ridiculous it all was the more difficult it was to get on with the job in hand (literally). It was one of the worst situations I've ever been in.

I had to, ahem, get? Put? I don't know what the right phrase is . . . Anyway, my sperm ended up in a plastic container, and then after I left someone went and collected it and that was that. It was all over quite quickly. Although not as quickly as I'd have liked, obviously.

The first op I had was on the hydrocele and I was completely knocked out for that. I won't go into too much detail but they turned the sac inside out so it released all of the pressure and then flattened it back down. They had to cut into my testicle, so I've got a little scar on there now.

They first tried to treat the varicocele with keyhole surgery. They went in through my groin as close to my testicle as possible and tried to clamp the vein. The hope was that would kill off the vein so the lump would go down. It was only under local anaesthetic so I was aware of everything that was going on, and it wasn't the most pleasant experience I've ever had.

Annoyingly that didn't work so they had to do another operation at Cheltenham General Hospital. This time they went in through what is effectively my love handle. Because there was so much muscle there it took ages to carve through it and it ended up taking three hours. Thankfully I was asleep for that one. They clamped the vein near my kidney, which stopped any more blood getting into the veins in my testicles, which meant the varicosity would eventually shrivel up and die. I was just praying it would work this time but it soon became clear that it hadn't.

I felt horrendous after that procedure and I could barely move my body. When I came round from the anaesthetic I was hallucinating like mad. I didn't know where I was – at one point I thought I was falling off a building. My friend came in to visit me and I was talking to him about stuff that happened years ago as if it was happening now, like my granddad did when he was unwell.

My family were sat around my bed and I was shouting at them and asking them what they were doing there because I didn't know what was going on. I was on a morphine drip and I was in so much pain I kept clicking the self-administering button to give myself more. I was off my nut.

Just like the first operation, that one didn't work. So all that pain was for nothing and I was gutted. I was referred to a hospital in Bristol to see a specialist and I had to go for three checks-ups before they could decide on the next step. They said the only thing they could do was operate once again and hope to God it worked this time.

For that op they cut through my groin and cut off the circulation to the vein for the third time. If that didn't work they were at a loss as to what they could do next.

When I came round from the operation I felt completely paralysed. It was as if I was being held down on the bed by someone with incredibly strong arms. I tried to turn my body over to get more comfortable but it was impossible.

I buzzed for a nurse to come in and asked him how I was supposed to go to the toilet, and he explained that I'd been fitted with a catheter because going on my own wouldn't be possible for a few days. It was so weird because you're constantly being drained of fluid but you don't know you're weeing. It was a very strange sensation.

I was in hospital for around a week and when I got home I still found it really hard to move around. It was the worst pain I've ever experienced. I can't even describe it. But looking back it was worth it because thankfully it was third time lucky and that op actually *worked*. It was such a relief. The whole process had taken over a year and it was horrible to have it all hanging over me for so long.

I was initially thinking I would only need one operation to get both of my bollocks sorted, but in the end it took four separate and very painful ones. I've now got three scars on my hip and lower torso area. One of them is about three inches long and about half an inch wide, straight across my pubic region. I've lost all sensitivity in that area so I can't feel it at all. It's totally dead around the scar, but it's not the worst thing that could have happened so I can live with it.

• • • • •

I worked at the solicitors from the age of nineteen until just after I turned twenty-four. It was a nine-to-five job and not the kind of thing I ever envisaged myself doing. I didn't mind the routine because at least I knew I could do my hours and leave, so I could plan when to go to the gym or see my mates. These days every work day is different so when people ask me what I've done the day before I really have to think about it. It takes me a good few minutes to remember because my life is pretty hectic.

I eventually left that job in early 2016 because I felt like I'd been there for long enough and it was time to move on and try something new. My next job was at a golf clothing company that partnered and sponsored various events. There was quite a lot of travelling involved but I quite enjoyed it, and it was refreshing after working such rigid hours. I didn't get a chance to properly get into it because I started there not long before I applied for *Love Island*, and as soon as I knew I'd secured a place in the show I quit my job.

• • • • •

I might get totally bollocked for saying this but I've got to be honest – before I went on the show I'd never, *ever* watched an episode of *Love Island* in my life. I didn't even really know what it was about.

Even when I flew out to Majorca and I was waiting to go into the villa I'd genuinely never seen a second of it, so I didn't know what to expect. It's a bit ridiculous that I didn't scour YouTube for clips so I knew what I was letting myself in for, but I think that probably would have made me more nervous.

I didn't know much about the structure of the show or what I'd have to do once I got in there, aside from what I'd been told during my meetings with ITV. I just thought it would be a laugh and one of those opportunities you should grab with both hands when it comes along.

It's not like I'd ever had this burning desire to do reality TV and kept a lookout for opportunities. I didn't have big dreams of becoming famous or making a name for myself. Even though I'd liked the idea of doing something in the entertainment industry when I was younger, I was pretty happy living my simple life in the country. To be honest the show probably came along at the right time. I reckon I needed a kick up the arse to do something different or I'd still be living with my parents when I was forty.

Considering I didn't know anything about *Love Island*, you're probably wondering why and how I ended up applying to go on the show. Let's just say that someone from the show got in touch with me via social media and encouraged me to try out for it. ITV have a network of scouts who look out for people who could work for certain shows. Sometimes they're out on the streets looking for people, sometimes they go to big events like The Clothes Show Live, and sometimes they'll look online and see if they can spot anyone who might fit the bill.

In my case I randomly got a message on Facebook in October 2016 from someone saying 'If you're interested in taking part in *Love Island* this year here's what you need to do.' Job done.

I applied online like tens of thousands of other people and I didn't think much of it. I honestly wasn't motivated by fame. I thought it would be a bit of a laugh, no one would see me on it and I'd be back home a couple of days after I went into the villa. I certainly didn't apply because I was desperately looking for love either. I didn't think I could go on a TV show and leave with a girlfriend.

About three or four weeks later I got a phone call from a London number . . .

When I answered, a girl called Lucy introduced herself and we chatted for a while. She said they'd read through my application and they wanted me to go down to the studios for an initial audition.

I told her I'd have to have a think and let her know because I still didn't really know if I wanted to do it. It would mean asking my boss to keep my job open for me, which he might not agree to do. And what if I hated it once I got into the villa? I ummed and ahhed and phoned Lucy back a couple of times to ask her some questions about when I'd have to leave home and how long I could potentially be away for, but I still wasn't convinced.

I mulled it over for a couple of days and I kept changing my mind about whether or not to go for it. In the end I thought 'What have I got to lose?' I was single at the time and it sounded like it could be quite a laugh. Even if I did manage to make it through the interview process it didn't mean I *had* to go on the show. If nothing else, going to the

ITV studios and meeting the telly execs would be a bit of an experience.

The first audition was at the ITV studios building near Waterloo. I went to the reception and explained what I was there for. I asked the receptionist if a lot of people were having interviews for *Love Island* that day and she laughed and said, 'Yes, and you'll be able to spot them all a mile off.' I looked over to the nearby seating area and clocked a group of guys wearing skinny jeans with their hair perfectly done. I thought, 'Yep, that'll be them, then.'

I was given a little sticker with my name on it and then I was shown to a room where about fifteen other guys were sitting. All the other lads were either from Essex or London, so I was the only country boy.

We all chatted a bit and I remember looking at them and thinking 'God, you're all well good-looking.'

Some of the guys clearly thought they'd got a place before they'd even started the process, but they were all really nice. Apparently a few of the guys who were in the group before us were so rude to people working on the show they were asked to leave. There's a big difference between arrogance and confidence and they obviously overstepped the mark.

After filling out a form we were called into an interview room one by one. I was fifth out of the fifteen so I didn't have to hang around for too long, thankfully. It would have been awful if I'd had to wait until the end.

They took a quick Polaroid of me so they could remember who I was, and then I walked into another room where two junior producers, one male and one female, were sat. There was a camera pointing right at my face and they started firing loads of questions at me.

I had to answer as naturally as possible. The girl sat at the back was making lots of notes so I did feel under pressure, but it's not in my nature to try to be clever or cocky. I was just myself and I answered everything really honestly. When the interview was over the producers said, 'Give us a month or so and if you haven't heard from us by then assume it's a no.'

I said my goodbyes, and of course the minute I left the room I thought of so many other things I could have said. It definitely could have gone better. I really didn't think it hadn't gone my way at all so I left feeling a bit disheartened.

When I got to the tube station I bumped into another one of the lads who had auditioned. He was really upbeat and said to me, 'I smashed it! I'm so happy. It could not have gone better. How about you?' I replied, 'It went all right I guess, but we'll see what happens.' Funnily enough he didn't end up getting picked. It's a shame because he was a nice guy.

I'd told my brother Tom and my best mate Charlie I'd applied for the show, but I didn't tell anyone where I'd been that day so I thought I'd be able to put it out of my head as soon as I stepped on the train home. But something kept niggling at me. I realised it was because I really did want to do the show if I was offered it.

I checked my emails every day after that because I wanted to know one way or another, but I didn't hear anything. I decided that no news was good news and I felt really excited. I was on a proper high and I even started going to the gym to get my body in better shape in case I got chosen. I became really motivated.

Finally one day I got an email from ITV saying 'Hi Chris. Thanks for coming in. Can you please complete another questionnaire for us?' In my head I was thinking, 'They wouldn't send me that unless I'm in with a good chance of getting through to the next stage.'

It was a bloody long questionnaire and I ended up having to complete it in three sittings because I wanted to give really good, long answers. I sent it off and waited to hear again. I waited. And waited.

I got a phone call thanking me for filling out the questionnaire and telling me that if I was successful in going forward they would be in touch in a couple of weeks. This whole thing was never-ending!

Two weeks went by and I didn't hear from them so I thought it was game over. But just to put my mind at rest, and so I could stop stressing about it, I phoned them to check. They explained that there had been a hold-up with the applications but they'd let me know the outcome soon. *More* waiting.

Finally – *finally* – in March 2017 one of the casting producers, Lewis, phoned me and he sounded really happy. That's definitely what you want to hear when you pick up a phone. People don't usually sound happy if they're going to give you shit news, do they?

Lewis was like, 'Mate, we saw your VT and loved it, and we also loved your questionnaire. We'd love you to come down and meet the three main executive producers and have a chat.' He gave me some potential dates and it was at that point they started booking my travel for me, and paying for it. Things were getting serious!

I felt so nervous the day I got the train to London for the big meeting. I met up with Lewis for a chat first, and then I was shown to a room where the execs were sat in a row looking at me. They started chatting to me and asking me various questions about myself. Again, I knew there was no point in trying to be someone I wasn't to impress them so I had a bit of a laugh with them. I probably said some stupid stuff but I don't remember a lot of it because I was so nervous.

The execs said they would aim to get back to me with a final yes or no by 5 May, which was another month away. I felt like the process was never going to end. Now I *really* wanted a place on the show and it made the waiting feel ten times as long.

When 5 May finally rolled around I was desperate to know the outcome. When the phone call came I took a deep breath and answered it . . . only to be told they still hadn't made up their minds. They said they'd get back to me in another week, so I geared myself up for another seven days of shitting myself.

Thankfully I didn't have to wait that long and a few days later a girl who worked on the show, Charlotte, called me. The conversation went like this:

'Hi, is that Chris?'

'Yes.'

'Oh hi, I'm calling from ITV. Just to say that we'd love you to be one of the bombshells on *Love Island* this year.'

'Seriously?'

'Seriously.'

· · · · ·

Shit.

· · · · ·

WICKED!

· · · · ·

Oh. My. God.

If I ruled the world

There are so many things I would do if I ruled the world. Firstly, I would help America out by sacking Trump and getting someone else in.

I'd also put people in stocks like they did in the olden days when they robbed people. I'd shame them into not doing it again.

I'd have the golfer Ian Poulter as my finance advisor because he's really good with business things. I'd also give my brother Ben a job because it would be funny to see what he came out with. He says some well stupid things. If nothing else he would make people laugh.

I'd have three-day weekends. No one should have to work on a Friday. And I'd increase wages to cover it. Everyone would be happy with that. Apart from maybe the people who have to pay them.

My office would be well plush with polar bear wallpaper and loads of polar bears kicking about all over the place. I think it would make people feel relaxed when they came in for meetings.

I'd set up water systems for camels in the desert. You see a lot of camels and sometimes they look really thirsty because it's very hot. I'd do the same for all people too, because I read that you can survive longer without food than you can without water.

I'd travel around using a jetpack. It's an easy mode of transport because there would be no traffic.

I'd wear a two-piece tracksuit. I feel like all the people who rule the world at the moment have to wear proper smart suits. I'd want comfort.

5

Great Kem-istry

I think that phone call from ITV was the best one I'd ever had. Charlotte asked me how I was feeling and I was like, 'I'm buzzing!' some 65,000 people had applied for the show and I'd got a bloody place.

She gave me a list of all the things they needed from me, including a load of paperwork and a copy of my passport. Because I was a bombshell she didn't know for sure when I would be joining the show, but I would still be flying out around the same time as the rest of the cast. *In less than a month.*

Bombshells are people who get dropped into the show at random times to mix things up a bit, and there was a small part of me that thought 'Why am I not in the villa from day one?' Then Charlotte said to me, 'Remember, Alex Bowen was a bombshell last year and he did amazingly. Some of the people who do the best in the show are the ones that come

91

in late. I think we want to put you in early on in the series but until it gets started we won't know.'

Work had no idea that I'd even applied for *Love Island*, so although I was over the moon about being offered a place on the show, I wasn't sure how I was going to tell my boss that I was quitting to join a reality show. In the end I was totally honest and he very kindly offered to keep my job open for me, in case I wanted to go back later on down the line.

I went for another meeting with ITV the following week to film my master interview, which is the video that is shown when you first go in, where you talk a bit about yourself and your background.

I also had a meeting with the execs and the head of journalism, who advises you about the press side of things and gives you an idea of what you can expect once you come out of the show. The execs told me that I was now a part of the *Love Island* family and they would do everything they could to protect me from the prying eyes of the tabloids.

They asked if there was anything scandalous I needed to tell them about my past that could come out once I joined the show. They explained that it wouldn't jeopardise my place on *Love Island*, but they needed to be aware of any potential scandals upfront. That way, if any stories did come out they could help to shut them down straight away.

My past is pretty chilled so there genuinely wasn't anything I was worried about. Victoria had been my only long-term girlfriend and we'd ended on good terms and I couldn't imagine her selling any stories. They would have been pretty boring anyway, to be fair.

· · · · ·

Once the meeting was over Lewis, one of the casting producers, walked me outside and said, 'We'll be in touch this weekend to get your flights booked.' Bloody hell, it was really happening.

I felt amazing on the journey home. It was such a good feeling to know that in a matter of weeks I was going to be sunning myself surrounded by gorgeous women. What a win.

I was only allowed to tell a couple of members of my family I was going into *Love Island* because it had to be kept really quiet. If it ended up being leaked to the press I would have lost my place and I could *not* chance that happening. Not after everything I'd been through.

It had taken so long to get to this point and now I was here I really wanted it. It had been a real buzz getting through each stage so I was so ready for it. I would have been absolutely gutted if anything had jeopardised it.

• • • • •

I was collected by a taxi at the end of May, although I can't remember the exact date now, and I flew out to Majorca the same afternoon. Along with everyone else who was going to be in the show, I immediately went into lockdown for ten days before the show started. My phone was taken off me the moment I got on the plane to Spain and I had no contact with friends and family from then on. In fact, my phone wasn't switched on again until I walked out of *Love Island* nine weeks later.

I was looked after by a chaperone called George, who was a great guy. Everyone who was joining the show was dotted around the island in different hotels to minimise the chances of bumping into each other.

All the chaperones were in a WhatsApp group, and every

time they took their cast member out they had to message everyone else to let them know where they were going.

It would have been a disaster if we'd seen each other before the show kicked off because they wanted totally natural reactions from everyone, and if we'd known what or who to expect that wouldn't have happened. You can never recreate a first reaction so it needed to be real and honest. It was all very covert and that added to the excitement.

I still didn't know much about how the show worked and I wasn't too fussed. I didn't ask George any questions because I decided to wait until I was in there to find out. I figured out little bits and pieces but nothing could have prepared me for how the show actually worked. Even if it had all been explained to me in detail it would still have been a million miles away from what I was expecting. I don't think anything can really prepare you for *Love Island*.

I did nothing other than sunbathe, go to the gym and eat in the run-up to joining the show. George and I were with each other constantly, but luckily we got on really well and we had a good laugh. I think I would have gone a bit mad if I'd been on my own the whole time.

Four days after the show started, George got a call from the show's producers saying I had to make my way to the casting villa with my suitcase, which I knew meant I was due to go into the main villa that day. I was originally supposed to go in on day four but it absolutely nailed it down and there were thunderstorms so it got postponed.

I'd already worked out what I was going to wear so at least that was sorted. It was essential that I looked good when I met the girls for the first time. I was also very aware that I was going to be seen on TV so I wanted to look on point for my big entrance. I wore some black jeans and a white shirt, which I was pleased about because I had a bit of a tan by then.

George had sent photos of several potential outfits to the series producer a couple of days before to make sure I wasn't wearing a similar outfit to any of the other contestants. I cleverly worked out that must mean I wasn't going in alone.

When I arrived at the casting villa my suitcase was given a final check over by security to make sure I didn't have anything dodgy in there. There was a list of items like scissors and tweezers that you weren't allowed to take in for safety reasons. Branded clothes were also banned, so nothing was allowed to have any kind of logo on it. I'd done a bit of shopping before I went in but I hadn't gone too crazy. I kind of wish I'd done more actually, but I knew we'd be spending a lot of time in shorts so I didn't think I'd need that much. I love clothes and I have a lot these days. Far more than I need, but I'm not complaining.

Everyone was very tight-lipped about what was going to happen next but I'd already worked out that I wouldn't be entering the villa solo. I wasn't nervous as such, but I was a bit on edge because I was heading into unknown territory. I was about to go and live with a group of people I'd never met and be filmed 24/7. This was *not* normal.

· · · · ·

I was mic'd up and about two minutes before I was due to enter the villa I was introduced to Jonny Mitchell. We had a quick chat about how weird the situation was, and then we both stood in the bedroom waiting to be given the nod to say we could walk out. I remember giving Jonny a high five and a cuddle, and then it was time . . .

It was such a surreal moment walking in and seeing all the girls. My head was all over the shop. I remember thinking all the girls looked amazing, but it was such a blur and I was so shell-shocked it was hard to properly focus on any of them.

The boys were all up on the balcony looking down at us, probably thinking 'Who do they think they are?' That made me feel quite weird because some of the girls had already coupled up with them so we became their rivals.

Funnily enough the first person I hugged was Olivia, which is mad looking back. I gave her a kiss on the cheek, and then I went and sat down with Camilla and Montana and had a chat. It was so hard to take it all in.

I spent the first few hours going round and talking to different girls, and I got on well with all of them. Some of them were already coupled up, which made things tricky. The girls who weren't at that time were Montana, Chloe and Camilla, so I knew I had to win one of them over if I wanted to stay longer than a few days.

When the first recoupling happened I didn't have any genuine feelings for anyone, but I wanted Chloe to pick me. It wasn't because there was any kind of spark between us. I wanted her to pick me so that I could stay in. I know that sounds out of order but I just didn't want to leave before I'd had a chance to enjoy the whole experience. Essentially you're not going to have any kind of chance to find love if you're in the villa for two days and then you get booted out.

At the end of the day it's a TV series and it is a bit of a game. The aim is to stay in there and give yourself a bit of an opportunity to do the best you can, and hopefully get together with someone you could build something genuine with.

As I've mentioned, I was pretty sceptical about meeting the love of my life in the villa and I was never going to force anything, but once I was in there I didn't see any harm in seeing if anything developed. If I did get together with someone I liked it would be a massive bonus, but I wasn't instantly drawn to anyone. I didn't have any real physical attraction with anyone until I realised there was this spark between Olivia and me.

Chloe did end up picking me, so that kept me in. It may sound harsh that that was the way I was thinking about it because Chloe was a really nice girl, but we weren't going anywhere romantically. I knew it wasn't one of those situations where I was going to catch feelings.

When it came to recoupling the following week I repaid the favour to Chloe and picked her, so I ended up being coupled with her for two weeks. We did kiss and stuff but I saw it as a bit of fun. Then I realised she was starting to like me a bit so I tried to keep my distance without appearing rude.

At one point she tried to have a serious conversation with me about 'us' and I didn't want to get into it. I was chilling on a beanbag and I didn't want to mug her off so I tried to take the discussion in a different direction. My mind literally went off on one because I did not want to have that kind of chat. I asked her if she ever felt like a polar bear, because I do sometimes. She got a bit annoyed and said I wasn't taking her seriously, so I had to tell her straight up that I wasn't in the mood for it.

People often ask why I think I'm like a polar bear, and my answer is that I feel like I'm a very rare species and I'm often in a world of my own, like I imagine they are. And I really like them because they're fluffy and cute. I wish I actually was a polar bear and I could hunt otters. Do I mean otters? Or walruses? Do walruses live in water? Maybe it's seals. It's something like that anyway.

• • • • •

People thought I was a bit cocky when I first went into the villa, and I can see why I may have come across like that. But it was only because I was feeling a bit out of my depth that I said ridiculous things sometimes. And some of what I came out with was also intended to be tongue-in-cheek.

When I said that all the girls liked me I didn't mean to sound like an arrogant twat. I was sitting on the sofa in the lounge waiting for Kem to come out of the toilet one afternoon and I laid my head back and said, 'Oh my God, every girl in this fucking villa fancies me.' But I was literally talking to myself and I forgot it was being filmed. It sounded as if I thought that situation was well stressful. Like having some girls fancying me was the worst thing in the world. It was ridiculous but I didn't mean to sound like I thought I was God's gift. No wonder people thought I was a dick.

I also told Montana I thought I was a nine and three-quarters out of ten for a bit of banter and she was like, 'No, you're not.' I thought that was brilliant. Montana was funny. She's really clever and she's got a good personality.

I didn't think about what I was saying and that's the problem. I don't think my thoughts process properly through my brain and stuff just comes out. Then afterwards I think 'Eh?' My mum even had to defend some of the things I'd said when she went on *This Morning*. But you know, shows like that choose the bits they want to show. I think for the first week or so they showed me at my worst and I was a bit of a panto-mime villain, but people soon saw the real me.

You genuinely do forget about the cameras so quickly. Almost straight away I felt like I was living a normal life in there. Honestly, I walked in there really conscious of the cameras and within less than two days I thought it was the most normal thing in the world being filmed twenty-four hours a day. I swear, no one ever did anything in the villa just because there were cameras everywhere. In my opinion, anyway.

I have no idea how many cameras were in the villa in total but they were everywhere. There were cameramen in there with hand-held cameras hidden in huts but we never saw them. All the cameras were really well hidden and they were dotted around places you would never think they would be. There was even one in the toilet. They weren't monitored so the crew didn't watch it, but it was there as a safety precaution in case something happened to someone.

There were literally hundreds of crew but we hardly had any contact with them. It was kept to the bare minimum and only when really necessary. We could speak to them if we really needed to but we were generally left to get on with things.

They certainly didn't set up any scenes for us or ask us to do things for dramatic effect, or ask to reshoot arguments or anything. We were left to our own devices and everything that happened was totally natural.

• • • • •

I haven't seen much of the show since I left the villa, but from what I've read about in the press there wasn't anything I wish they hadn't filmed. I was surprised at some of the stuff they showed. Kem and I did some really random shit and I didn't think they would include it but they bloody did. Like when we showered together and shaved each other's initials into our pubes. We were just being idiots; we weren't doing it for screen time.

Mine and Kem's bromance wasn't an instant thing. I'd say our friendship was more of a grower. We didn't really speak at all for the first few days, and then he randomly offered to cut my hair. It took about an hour and we chatted about all sorts. We had the same banter and we liked the same kind of things. It made me realise how similar we were and after that we were really tight.

We started telling each other everything and we supported each other. Even when things weren't good with the girls we knew we had each other to speak to about it.

You have a lot of downtime in the villa and we would do literally anything to occupy ourselves. One day we went upstairs to the dressing room and got hold of some of the girls' make-up pots. We started playing curling with them in the bedroom like we were in a really shit Olympics. We ended up playing it for two hours. We always seemed to find funny, ridiculous things to do together. We were like a couple of kids in a very odd, surreal situation. The way we acted wouldn't have looked out of place in a primary school.

Kem and I both like our rap and grime music and we know a fair bit about it. Every time we were allowed a bit of music on in the villa, which was very rare, there would always be a bit of grime and we'd rap along. We were having a long conversation about it one day and we started rapping random shit together.

We'd made up loads of raps by the time we left, and of

course we also rapped in the end-of-series talent show, but we were robbed of the win by Alex and Jamie, who performed an acoustic song together, and Amber and Olivia, who put together a comedy roast. So we weren't just beaten by one couple, we were beaten by two.

We had a laugh all the time and by the time we left the villa I felt like Kem had been in my life for years. We were proper best mates. It was never awkward between us and we didn't ever have an argument. It is weird when you spend that much time with someone because you'd think we'd at least have disagreements, but we totally got each other.

I loved doing all the challenges because they were another way to fill time. Some of them were well funny, although we did have to do some ridiculous things too. The challenge team did an unreal job. I won the first challenge I did, the best body one, and I don't know how because I was up against people like Harley, who is an absolute unit. The girls had to choose using touch alone so maybe I was nice and smooth or something? I liked the obstacle course challenge with the paint water bombs and it was funny when the couples had to answer questions about each other, even though Olivia and I lost, which meant I got dunked a few times.

The only one I didn't take part in was the stripping challenge. People thought it was because I was upset because Olivia and I had a big argument when Muggy Mike came back into the villa, but the truth was I was really ill. I spent eight hours in hospital that day.

I'd slept in the lounge the night before and it was boiling hot in there. Despite that, I was shivering and feeling terrible. I couldn't get warm no matter what I did. I thought I probably had really bad sunstroke. I threw up all that morning and eventually the crew called a medic in to check me over. I couldn't keep anything down, not even water, so they took me to the local hospital and ran some tests.

They checked my blood and I had to give a urine sample so they could monitor my hydration levels. When they got the results back they showed that I was severely dehydrated and they gave me some medicine to drink that was supposed to replenish the water and salts in my body.

I couldn't even keep that down so they had to put me on a drip. But as soon as it finished I threw all the liquid back up. They put me on a second one and the same thing happened, so they had to put me on four hour-long drips and give me some anti-sickness medication.

Thankfully they did the job and I started to feel better. The hospital released me and I went back to the villa and went straight to bed. Kem came in and gave me a hug and told me he missed me, which was very sweet, and thankfully I bounced back pretty quickly. It was horrible though. I tend to get quite low when I feel ill and I hated not being with everyone else. Instead I was in bed feeling a bit teary.

I would say I got on with everyone in the villa. I had the fallout with Muggy Mike but I didn't see it as a massive deal. The guy's got no personality and he has nothing to say for himself so he didn't really bother me. It was annoying when he thought he was getting one over on me because Olivia admitted she found him attractive, but at the end of the day when she had to choose between me and Mike at the recoupling she went with me.

I'm pissed off I ever gave him the name Muggy Mike because it's become his trademark now. To be fair, it's the only interesting thing about him. If he didn't have that he would be known as Boring Mike. He's the driest human being I've ever met.

I know some people on social media said it would have been karma if Muggy Mike nicked Olivia from me because I'd nicked her from Sam, but I don't agree. I didn't *steal* Olivia. We didn't speak that much when I first went into the villa, and then one day we had a chat and we got on really well.

· · · · ·

It all happened the day Tyne-Lexy and Gabby came in as bombshells. They both had to choose two boys to cook a starter and a main course for them and then they got to go on a date with them. Tyne-Lexy chose Dom for the starter and me for the main, and Gabby chose me for the starter and Marcel for the main.

Dom, Marcel and I were all in the kitchen preparing the food and Dom said to me, 'Look, I've got to ask you. What do you think of Liv?' I said something like, 'Yeah, she's sound, but I don't really speak to her.' Then he told me she liked me and I was so taken aback I started giggling like a schoolboy.

I've never, ever not picked up on something like that before, but the more I thought about it the more it made sense. I had caught her looking at me more than usual that day and she kept laughing at everything I said.

Dom had just dropped the news on me and then I had to go on dates with two new girls, when all I really wanted to do was go and chat to Olivia some more. I wasn't interested in Tyne-Lexy or Gabby and all I could think about during the meals was Olivia.

Liv and I ended up having a really nice chat and even though she was coupled with Sam, she was making it pretty clear that she liked me. I didn't make a move or anything but other people in the villa could see there was an attraction between us. It filtered back to him and he started asking people if I'd been going behind his back and being snakey.

That night when Sam and I were round the fire pit he went off on one and made out like I'd snaked him. He thought I'd gone behind his back and cracked on with Liv, but all we'd done was have a conversation. Liv didn't ever want to be with Sam so it's not like they were in some committed relationship and I bowled in there and ruined it all. There was nothing to ruin.

That argument with Sam was a bit ridiculous. I got up in his grill and he told me not to. End of. That's all there was to it. He's quite fiery but I like him. He's a good bloke. We were sweet the following day and we're still totally fine now.

I also ended up having an argument with Amber in the villa, but I maintain that wasn't my fault. Quite early on when Kem and I were starting to become good mates, Kem took me aside and said that Amber had told him I'd given her a hug after Chloe picked me for recoupling, which was true. But she also claimed I said to her, 'Oh that's a relief. I'm here.' Amber tried to make out that I'd said it in a flirty 'I'm here for you' way, but that didn't happen. I would never have said 'I'm here' to her, and I would never have cracked on. I just thought 'Nah, I'm not having this,' so I decided to have it out with her.

I find it really hard to bite my tongue when things like that happen, and I was so angry about it. I couldn't understand why she'd said it. She was sat in the smoking area so I went over and confronted her. She was properly loud and ranty with me and refused to back down. I said to her I knew she was using me to wind Kem up and it was out of order.

At the end of the day, she knew that out of all the boys Kem would be most jealous of me, so she tried to use me. I didn't want any part of that shit. She wanted a reaction out of Kem so she could gauge how much he liked her, so she dragged me into it. I overheard Amber talking about it to some of the girls in the dressing room later on that day and I got really wound up so I challenged her on it again. It all kicked off for the second time and it was well uncomfortable.

In the end I was proved right. They showed a clip of the hug on *Aftersun* and everyone could see that I hadn't said anything to Amber, so I felt like I'd been vindicated (good word). Amber and I are sound now though. She's my mate and it was just one of those things. Things did get pretty heated in the villa at times because we were together all the time and there was no escape, but it was all forgotten really quickly too.

• • • • •

I was very lucky that my anxiety wasn't too bad while I was on *Love Island*. It's such an unnatural way to live and I guess that could have kicked off some kind of reaction in me, but I felt pretty level most of the time. I didn't love it when things kicked off in there but I handled it.

It was such a different environment from anything else I'd experienced and I had so much stuff going on in my head I was constantly distracted.

I guess it was a bit like when I was working as a conveyancer every day and my brain was being filled with facts and figures. This was similar, only my brain was filled with tasks, and wondering whether or not I'd make it through the next recoupling.

Because I had no idea what was going on in the outside world or back home those external factors couldn't have a negative influence on me. And although I went through the emotional wringer with Olivia on many occasions, which we'll come on to, I guess in a weird way at least all the drama in the villa kept me focused.

• • • • •

We honestly didn't have a clue about anything that was going on in the outside world where we were in the villa. Incredibly, I didn't know about the Grenfell Tower disaster until two weeks after I left the show. I heard someone mention it in a conversation and I was horrified when I found out what had happened. We'd been so sheltered, and when we came out I didn't really get the chance to sit down and catch up on all the news, so some stories filtered through to us at quite strange times.

We would have been notified if anything bad had happened to a family member or friend, but aside from that we were totally oblivious. Even now there are probably things that happened while I was away that I still don't know about.

The show's producers don't want you to know what's going on in the real world because they want you to be as natural and carefree as possible. They want you to be you and have your mind on the moment, and things that wouldn't matter if you were living your everyday life become much more significant.

You don't even know the time while you're in the villa. The only things that had the time on them were the phones the crew gave us so they could send us text messages, but they muddle up the times on every one of them so we only knew when it was time for dinner because of where the sun was.

We didn't know what time we were going to bed or what time we were getting up. Not that it mattered much to me because I was always the last one out of bed. Every now and again the crew would shout things at me like, 'It's not *Sleep Island*, get up!' Those beds were so comfy I could have slept and slept, but sadly that doesn't make for great TV.

I didn't mind being cut off from 'normal' life. You're pre-warned it's going to be like that before you go in so you are kind of prepared. I just accepted I wasn't going to be able to communicate with my family and friends. It's not like we were locked up either. If anyone had asked to leave they would have been allowed. There weren't high fences and razor wire surrounding the entire villa.

There was never a moment when I even considered leaving. Even when things got tough it didn't cross my mind that I could quit and run back to normal life. The vibe was so good that even if I was feeling worn out, the energy would lift me back up. I'll never forget that feeling. Even now there are times when I really miss it. They were such good times. I liked that I didn't have a phone because it meant that I wasn't distracted all the time. And that even though there was quite a lot of drama, life was pretty simple and easy. We were very protected in there and I enjoyed that.

It's a date

What's your idea of a good date?

I haven't been on many dates in my life but a good one would be doing something like go-karting so it's not standard and boring. I think you should go out of your comfort zone and do something different. If you're doing something active it avoids any awkwardness because you've just got to crack on.

Who would be a nightmare date for you?

Someone who struggled to express any emotions. Someone dull, basically. I would hate to be stuck on a date with someone who didn't have anything to say for themselves.

Are looks or personality more important to you?

Personality, definitely. With every girl I've ever fallen for it's been her personality first. I've seen really nice-looking girls around in the past but not thought much of them because I don't know them. But once you get to know someone, that's when you properly fall for them. I would much rather be with someone who was less good-looking but really funny than be with the best-looking girl in the world who has got nothing to offer.

Have you ever been on any awkward dates where you've wanted to leave and can't?

Not really, because I've always got to know girls before we've been out. Like, I'll have met them in the pub and chatted to them and known they're all right. I've learned a bit about them early on.

Have your mates been on any awful dates?

A lot of my mates are on dating apps and some of them jump in well quickly and then wonder why they get into tricky situations. One of my mates went on a date with a girl recently and told me the following day that he was in love with her. It was well funny.

What's the worst way a girl has knocked you back?

This is going to sound so muggy but I've not experienced it that often. I've had girls who have not replied to messages I've sent them and stuff. In fact, some of the girls who didn't get back to me before I went into *Love Island* tried to slide back in after I went on the show. Obviously I was with Olivia by then, but I would never have gone there anyway.

How do you knock girls back if you're not interested?

To be fair, I don't mind it if girls come on a little bit strong and I'll always give them a chance. I think boys secretly like it if girls are really forward. It doesn't scare me, and I'm always polite if I'm not interested.

If you were single and in a club what would put you off a girl?

If she was in the middle of a dance floor slut-dropping. I also like less make-up on girls rather than too much. I'd rather be able to see what a girl actually looks like. It's also weird when girls edit themselves so much on Instagram they don't look real. I know that my mates have been caught out when they've met up with a girl and she's turned up looking nothing like she does in her pictures. Why would you try to trick someone? They're going to find out what you look like eventually!

6

No Man is an Island

When Olivia and I first started to like each other I was still coupled with Chloe and she was obviously still coupled with Sam. It was the boys' turn to pick first at the next recoupling, so of course I was always going to go for Liv. Only Muggy Mike got in there first. He knew I liked her but he's not the kind of person to let something like that stand in his way. Also, I won't deny there was a bit of an attraction between Liv and Mike. Olivia and I were just getting to know each other so we didn't have any kind of commitment, but I was still gutted. Thankfully Chloe picked me again so I was able to stay on the island.

· · · · ·

The week when Olivia was coupled with Mike was hard, but we liked each other more and more each day so all I could do was hold out for the next coupling and hope we got a chance to get together.

Before the next coupling happened Tyla came in as a bombshell, and all the guys thought she was gorgeous. I was already falling for Liv but I felt like she was playing Mike and me off against each other a bit at times and I didn't like that.

Tyla made it pretty clear from the word go that she was interested in me and it was the first time the shoe was on the other foot. I had a bit more control and it was my chance to test the waters and see if Olivia really did care about me. Tyla and I were having a laugh and getting a bit flirty but Liv was playing it really cool. Then she came up and collared me outside the bedroom, and that's when I knew for sure it was bothering her.

It was the girls' turn to pick that night and Olivia told me straight that I had to ask Tyla not to pick me. I was quick to remind her that when it was the boys' turn to pick and I knew Mike was going to pick her she didn't say anything to him to stop him. She told me that things had changed since then and then she started crying. I was really shocked because it was the first time she'd shown any proper emotion in the villa. She admitted it was the first time she'd cried in a year and a half, and that's when I knew it was serious.

Olivia had made her feelings for me very clear but I still wasn't about to bow down to her and run straight over to Tyla and beg her not to couple with me. I didn't want her to think she could tell me what to do and I'd obey her like a lapdog. In the end I left it until just before the recoupling and then asked Tyla not to pick me, which was a big risk.

I knew whoever Tyla picked that night had immunity from the next recoupling, which was an incentive for people to couple up with her. But I knew it was only right that I did what Olivia asked. In the end Tyla picked Dom, and it was a bloody relief when Liv picked me.

After that, things between Olivia and me went from strength to strength. Yes, we fell out a lot, but the good times were amazing. The thing about being in somewhere like *Love Island* is that everything is magnified. It's so intense. You go from not knowing a group of people to living with them every day. You would never move in with someone you like straight away, but Liv and I were living with each other before we'd even said hello to each other.

The usual way to get together with someone is to go on a date for a couple of hours, or go to one of your houses and talk and chill out. You don't start sharing a bed and spending pretty much every waking moment with them. A week in the villa is like a month in the real world because so much happens in a short space of time.

· · · · ·

It was really hard when us boys were taken out of the normal villa and put in Casa Amor with the five new girls. Olivia and I had only coupled up for the first time six days before but not for one second did I think about cheating on her. I also completely trusted her not to crack on with any of the new guys back in our villa. By that point we already had a solid bond and I would never have done something behind her back.

It was such a weird twist taking us out. It was fucking mad, really. I know it probably made good TV but it was well harsh. I think all the boys were worried about their girls to a certain extent. Even Marcel was screwy about Gabby. We all knew Gabby completely respected Marcel and would never have done anything but he was freaking out. There were times when we ended up laughing about how awful the situation was, otherwise we would have cried.

Even though I was pretty confident Liv would stay faithful to me, there was always a chance I'd walk back into the villa and find that she'd hooked up with another guy. I won't lie, I was nervous.

If I'd chosen to couple up with a girl from Casa Amor and Olivia had chosen to be with one of the new guys back in the villa we would both have been safe. But if only one of us had picked someone new the other person would immediately get dumped from the island.

If neither of us picked someone else and we chose to be with each other, we would also both be safe. So we had to trust each other not to choose to be with someone else. It was tough and a real game changer and it was purely a trust thing.

I had to do what my heart told me to do and I honestly thought Olivia would do the same. I was standing in the bedroom waiting to re-enter the villa and I knew it was make or break time. That was when I started shitting myself.

The lads reassured me that everything would be fine, but we'd been away for three days, which feels like so much longer in there. So much can happen in that time. When I walked into the garden and saw that Olivia was on her own I had the biggest smile on my face. That was such an amazing moment.

· · · · ·

I started caring a lot for Olivia really quickly. Even when I was pissed off with her or I didn't like some of the things she was doing, I still liked her so much. Or if I was annoying her and she was getting narked with me, I wanted to make it better straight away. Even though the way she acted hurt me at times, like when she admitted she'd like a bit with Mike and I felt mugged off, I wanted to stick with it. I didn't ever think 'Fuck this shit, it's not worth it.'

It was when I began getting proper feelings for Olivia that things started to get emotionally tough. When you genuinely like someone and you know that someone could choose to take your girl away from you it feels horrible. It's such a weird environment. Imagine if you were dating someone you really liked in the real world and someone walked up to you and said they were going to take her out on a date and there was nothing you could do about it. It does your head in. It sent me a bit insane. It's really hard. Especially as all the guys fancied Olivia. I couldn't get her off my mind.

As anyone who saw the show knows, it wasn't exactly plain sailing between Liv and me and we had our fair share of rows. Sometimes that was so hard because we couldn't escape from each other. It's not like we could go for a long walk to cool off.

The lie detector test was a real low point for me. I asked Liv during it if she actually loved me and she took it really badly. She thought I was testing her, and I guess I was. She was so upset she was raging and she said, 'I would have said yes but I fucking hate him at the minute so I'm going to say no.' That was the only question I really cared about and I was really upset by her answer. I didn't know if we'd be able to pull things back after that.

We had a chat afterwards and I explained to her that I only

115

asked her that question because I was given the opportunity to. I wasn't having a go at her, it was for my peace of mind, and I explained that. I spoke like an adult and tried to stay as level-headed as possible. It took a while but we worked it out. We always seem to manage to come back from the bad stuff.

One day all the couples had a brunch together and Liv said to me, 'I feel in general that you don't like that I'm loud, the way that I speak, the way that I dress, that's how I feel, Chris.' I felt so bad. I would never want her to feel like that. It wasn't the case at all. Quite the opposite. But maybe I wasn't expressing myself very well.

I said to her, 'I'm telling you, if that's the way I make you feel, if you feel like it's me who is dragging you back or holding you back or if you feel like you're acting differently around me, then you can't be with me. You need to do it for yourself. As much as that hurts. I want you to be happy and if you're telling me that when you're around me, you can't be you, then that is rubbish.'

Even as I was saying the words I was hoping she wasn't seriously thinking that we couldn't be together any more. It hurt that she felt like that, but it would have hurt a lot more if she'd walked away from me.

The whole Stormzy drama was difficult too. He tweeted saying he didn't think Olivia was good enough for me, and my first thought was that I was gassed that he's tweeted about me! Stormzy knew who I was! My second thought was 'I had better calm down here and not look so excited because he's just slagged off Liv.' That incident also caused a massive argument between us but it was just his opinion and I wasn't to blame for his point of view.

There were days when Olivia and I argued non-stop, and

there were times when I'd be in bed bawling my eyes out because it really got to me. We were trying to make a relationship work and there were so many negative factors having an influence. I felt like I was constantly on edge and really overwhelmed. When things build up inside me I do break down and that happened on several occasions.

I don't mind the fact that people saw me crying on camera at all. I am an emotional person and I don't hide that. I don't dress up how I'm feeling. If I'm happy, I smile. If I'm sad, I cry. I've never been someone who slaps on a smile and cracks on when they're feeling crap. I can't stop my emotions coming out.

I guess my emotions were running so high because I knew I'd caught feelings for Liv and there was no going back. I really wanted things to work but sometimes it felt like we were on the brink of giving up and there was nothing I could do to stop it.

The first time I told Olivia I loved her she gave me a load of shit for it, which slightly ruined the moment. We were sitting on the balcony and I said to her, 'I love you to pieces,' and she replied, 'You love your mum to pieces.' It wasn't really the romantic moment I was hoping for and I wondered if I'd made a mistake being so upfront about my feelings. But luckily it wasn't long before she opened up too.

The moment when Olivia asked me to be her boyfriend was one of my best times in *Love Island*. It was so cute. I wasn't expecting it at all. We were sat on the balcony one evening and she listed ten things she liked about me, like the fact my eyes made me look like a husky and I made her want to be a nicer person.

She explained that past relationships had affected her and she had a lot of baggage, but she was working on it. Then she asked me if I wanted her to be my girlfriend and it was the sweetest thing.

It was the first time I'd seen the real her. She'd totally opened up and spent time deciding what to write and she'd put in real effort, and it was such a nice feeling. Everything that built up to that moment felt like it was worth it.

. . . . .

One of the most life-changing things that happened to me in the villa was becoming a dad to baby Cash. I love that boy and he's a good-looking lad. It was such a strange thing to experience and it made me realise what bloody hard work it is having a baby.

I don't know why I got so emotional over him but I felt really attached and like it was a common bond Liv and I had. It was bare weird but it made me think about what it would be like if we had our own kids one day. I feel well sad that looks like it won't happen now, but for the moment Cash is staying with me and its nice having him in my flat.

We weren't allowed to take Cash with us when we left *Love Island* because those dolls cost about £1,800 to replace. But he was at the *Love Island* reunion party, which we went to just after we got back home, so we put him in Liv's bag when no one was looking and took him home. The execs know I've got him now but no one's asked for him back yet so I reckon I've got away with it. They couldn't take him away now anyway. It would be like taking an actual kid away. I reckon he'd go for a fortune if we put him on eBay but we could never part with him. I've even got him some new clothes. I don't care if that's odd. He's my boy.

. . . . .

Because everything in mine and Liv's relationship was on fast forward, we ended up meeting each other's families really quickly when they came to the villa towards the end of the series. Liv's mum and sister arrived to see her and I got on really well with both of them. Her mum is literally a dream. I love her to pieces. She used to give me the biggest hugs whenever I saw her. She seemed to properly care for me. I'll really miss them all.

My family also adore Olivia. They thought the world of her from the first moment they met and she became a part of our family. Her and my mum sit down and have proper deep conversations. My mum told her stuff even I didn't know about our family.

· · · · ·

When the final approached I was looking forward to it but I absolutely was not expecting to win. I had a strong feeling it was going to be Kem and Amber. We got to see some of the public's comments during several of the challenges and mine and Olivia's weren't always favourable. Some people loved us, but some people hated parts of our relationship. Some people liked me and didn't like Olivia, and some people didn't like me and liked Olivia. I guess we were quite divisive, and the fact we argued a lot probably didn't help. I also think it's only now we're out that people can see how relatable we are, and also how much we mean to each other.

As a couple, Kem and Amber were solid and fun and really likeable. They didn't have too many ups and downs and they were very sweet together. I was pretty confident they were always going to take the trophy. And I do think they deserved it.

The thing with shows like this is that it's nice to come

first but in a way it doesn't really matter who does. It's the same with *The X Factor* or *Britain's Got Talent*. It doesn't define your abilities or stop you doing what you want to do.

I genuinely wasn't disappointed. If you'd told me a year ago I'd be in *Love Island* at all, let alone get to the final, I'd have thought you were mad. So to have got that far was incredible. I mean, how many people can say they've been on a show like that? I took an incredible girlfriend and a best mate away from it, so I feel like a bloody winner.

· · · · ·

I think it was during the final that I first realised my life was about to change pretty dramatically because that was when we got a sense of how big the show had been back in the UK. All the people who were there were so excited about it and there was a real buzz among all the crew. It felt like it had been a huge deal. Then the producers sat us all down and told us how much of a success it had been and what we should be prepared for over the coming weeks.

The wrap party was a real laugh and we got to meet a lot of the people who had been working behind the scenes. Everyone got boozed and then we headed back to the casting villa to carry on. We were all on such a high. I eventually got to bed at 6 a.m. and then we had to get up to fly back to London at 10 a.m. the same day. I did *not* feel good.

· · · · ·

When we got given our phones back I turned mine on and it went crazy. I had loads of old messages from friends from weeks earlier saying 'Why aren't you replying to me?' They thought I'd been ignoring them until they saw me on TV. So then I had loads of messages saying 'Why didn't you bloody tell me you were going on *Love Island*?'

The first thing I wanted to find out about was what had been happening with my friends and family. One of my mates, Tim, got married and I had to miss the wedding because of the show, which was a shame. The press spotted some pictures of me on his stag do on social media the week before I went into *Love Island* so they phoned him and asked if he wanted to sell any stories on me. They also did it to five or six of my other friends, but no one was tempted. As I've said before, I haven't got any skeletons in my closet anyway.

I know who my proper mates are but a lot of people have come crawling out of the woodwork since I left *Love Island*. People I hadn't spoken to for years started dropping me a line. I don't follow that many people on Instagram and if someone you don't follow messages you those messages go into a request folder. I checked that folder after I came out of the show and no word of a lie I was getting two or three messages a second, which is a crazy amount. I got messages from people I would never have heard of in my life if I hadn't gone on *Love Island*. I had over 900,000 messages on my feed. Obviously you can't read them all. There are only so many hours in the day.

I've got so many unread messages because I can't keep up with them. The minute you reply to someone you get another one back, so you're in exactly the same position! I don't think I'll ever clear all my messages because it's so hard to keep up with things.

Every time I wrote a post I got so many comments. I was

only used to getting a few from my mates so it was quite overwhelming. It's nice to hear from people, but you do get a lot of people asking you to help them out with things. I've had a lot of requests from people asking me to mention their club night or their products. And I don't want to be a dick about it but if I did everything I was asked I wouldn't have time to breathe.

It's such a tricky thing because if you say no to things you can come across like you think you're something special, but that's not the case at all. If I post about everything I'm asked to people will start thinking my Instagram page is a business one and I really want to keep it as real as possible for fans as well as myself.

I also want my social media to be interesting and not just a showcase for promotions. People like me because I'm just a normal person and I don't want it to be all sell, sell, sell. Everyone who asks for a favour doesn't realise that twenty other people have probably asked me that day. If you do it for one, everyone else will be like 'Then why on earth wouldn't you do it for me?' At the end of the day it's easier not to do any at all, which is a shame. I'm constantly apologising to people for not being able to help out. I've had to toughen up a lot in that respect because I really don't like letting people down or upsetting them.

• • • • •

I thought I would be much more aware of what people at home were thinking of me when I was in the villa, and also concerned about what had been said about me in the press. But once I got out I just wasn't that bothered. The only person I'd been worried about was my mum. She doesn't like me swearing and I do swear a lot, and I also smoked in the villa, which she hated. I don't actually smoke usually but everyone else was having one and I fancied it so I joined in.

There was a debate about smoking on *Love Island* in the bloody House of Lords, and even though I smoked the least out of everybody the picture they used to illustrate it was of me. So Theresa May was sat looking at a photo of me with a fag hanging out of my mouth while everyone discussed whether or not we were a bad influence on the younger generation.

Strangely, one thing my mum wasn't that bothered about was me having sex on TV. I wasn't planning to do it. In fact, I was going to actively avoid it. But then it just sort of . . . happened. I was lucky because the producers didn't show a lot of Olivia and me getting it on.

Liv spoke about it once when she was on the balcony with the girls, but it wasn't made out to be a big deal, and I was really grateful for that. Kem and Amber were shown getting down to it a lot, which I know they weren't thrilled about once they got out.

While we're on the subject of sex I also just want to set the record straight about something – I did not actually ask for extra-large condoms while I was in the villa. What happened was that Liv and I were in bed one night and I'd taken my microphone off. Olivia and I were talking about how I couldn't get the condoms on and because there were microphones in the headboards the crew overheard us. The following morning I got called to the beach hut and a member of the crew said they were getting a special delivery for me. When I got back to the villa these large condoms had magically appeared in my drawer.

My willy did become a bit of a talking point in the villa. And the same thing happened on the outside when some naked photos of me were leaked. A male crew member sent some pictures of me to his mates, along with a message saying 'This is what I have to look at every day.' One of his friends leaked them to the press and all of a sudden they were on every website and in every magazine and newspaper going.

After the show finished we all sat down with members of the crew and they briefed us about everything that had gone on. Sarah, one of the execs, explained to me that the pictures had leaked and she apologised. She said that they'd done their best to remove them from certain sites, but they only had so much power. I don't know if the guy who sent the message ended up getting sacked, but I very much doubt he'll get a promotion any time soon.

To be fair, it's not a terrible thing that everyone knows I've got a big willy, but it's weird that complete strangers were talking about it. It's a bit odd that people I don't know were talking about it on social media.

The craziest thing was when I went to a friend's wedding after I left the island. I was sat in the church before the ceremony and one of my friend's girlfriends turned to me and said, 'I've got a naked photo of you on my phone.' I mean, what do you say to that? I laughed and replied, 'How nice for you!'

Even though I smoked and swore, Mum was still my biggest cheerleader. She said that everyone back home in the Cotswolds had been supporting me too, and she couldn't go anywhere without people asking her about *Love Island*. She got a phone call from one of my cousins the night I went in saying she'd spat her tea everywhere when I walked onto the screen because she was so shocked.

Some friends of my parents went out to dinner at a really nice restaurant one night and they asked the owner to put *Love Island* on so they could watch me. They didn't miss a single episode. Mum also bumped into an 87-year-old lady in our local supermarket. I've known her since I was about ten because I used to play football with her grandson and she said to my mum, 'I've been watching my little Chrissy. I wouldn't miss the show for the world. What's the point in being a prude at my age?' She even admitted she'd cried when she saw me crying over Olivia, bless her.

• • • • •

I don't think the enormity of what I'd been through properly hit me until I got back to the UK. We all did bits of press on the plane home, and when we landed back at Gatwick airport *that's* when we realised that *Love Island* was an even bigger deal than we'd thought. It wasn't just a bit popular, it was fucking massive. It was crazy. We were being treated like we were a bunch of athletes being welcomed back after winning loads of medals.

There were masses of people with banners screaming and asking for autographs. I'd never signed an autograph before in my life.

There were so many people there to greet us it was really overwhelming. I couldn't move without someone, whether it was a pap or a member of the public, taking a photo of me. I'd had cameras focused on me every single day in the villa, but this was on a totally different level because these ones were in my face and there was no escaping them.

The month before I'd got on a plane as a complete unknown, and now I was walking through the arrivals hall with a group of new mates and being greeted by a wall of fans. Bloody hell, I'd become a celebrity.

The weirdest things I said in the villa and why

'What's the most common owl in Britain? Tea T'owl.'

I told Olivia that joke and I think she was honestly impressed. It's been kicking about for years so I must have heard it somewhere and thought 'I like that' and it stayed with me. It's true though, innit!

'Jason Staythumb.'

I was asked to guess Chloe's celebrity crush during one of the tasks and I wrote Jason Staythumb. It was the right answer because she fancies Jason Statham, I just didn't know how to spell his name so I wrote it how it sounds. I got the point though, which is the main thing.

'Dip your carrots in the hummus.'

This was a silly conversation that Kem and I had and essentially it was about shagging. And hummus.

'I'm like an Easter egg which has been fridged for too many days. You won't crack me.'

You know when you've had an Easter egg in the fridge for ages and it goes rock hard and you can't break the thing? I felt just like that. I didn't want to let anyone crack me.

'Garlicio, garlicio?'

I said this to the owner of a food shop when Olivia and I went shopping. I just thought I had to put an 'o' on the end of all words so Spanish people would understand what I was talking about.

7

Living the Dream

We were still contracted with ITV for a week after the show finished, which basically meant they were like our employers. After that we were on our own, and it was up to us if we wanted to get agents or managers and try to take things to the next level.

I think everyone had been thinking about trying to carve out a career in the entertainment industry because of course we were being presented with an amazing opportunity. In a matter of weeks we'd all gone from being complete unknowns to being recognisable faces, and we were keen to make the most of it.

I didn't know how it all worked and how you go about signing up with an agency, but I'd already arranged to meet a couple of guys called Jim and Chris from a management company called Off Limits.

They'd got in touch with my parents within a few weeks of me going on *Love Island* and explained that although they would actively look around for work for me, it would be up to me to decide whether or not I wanted to sign with them once I left.

They were taking a bit of a risk putting in the hours to land me paying jobs because they had no idea if I would choose to stick with them. All that effort would have gone to waste if I'd decided I liked another company better.

I travelled straight from Gatwick airport to the Park Plaza Hotel in Waterloo where I was due to meet Chris and Jim that evening. Most of the cast were staying in the same hotel so it was like being back in the villa sometimes. Only without any cameras and with a lot more freedom.

I had a couple of hours to chill out and then I headed down to the bar for what I thought would be a quiet chat. When I arrived the whole place was swarming with various management companies that were desperate to talk to the *Islanders* in the hope that they could sign them up.

I introduced myself to Chris and Jim and we immediately began chatting. I felt comfortable with them straight away because they weren't giving me the hard sell. They explained what they could do for me but they didn't pressure me at all.

While I was talking to Jim and Chris another manager came up and collared me to ask if he could speak to me. I stepped away to hear what he had to say and the first thing he did was slag off Chris and Jim, which immediately made me feel defensive. I thought 'There's no way I'm going to sign with you now.' You shouldn't have to put other people down just to prove yourself or get what you want. Your abilities should speak for themselves.

The other manager was giving me all these reasons that I should sign with him, and he was suggesting all the different things we could do career-wise. I'm not going to lie; some of them were well dodgy. It was all very much about making a quick buck and a lot of it involved me stripping off, which wasn't the way I wanted to go. Yes, I'd been wandering around in a pair of swimming shorts for several weeks while I was on the show, but I didn't want to become known as some kind of 'rent a body'. There's a lot more to me than that.

I spoke to another four or five agents that night but I knew from Jim and Chris's approach that I liked them and we would work well together. It felt like all the other managers were trying to sell me a dream, but Chris and Jim were very grounded and honest. I felt very comfortable with them, and I certainly didn't with everyone I met. You've got to be able to be open with a manager without feeling awkward in any way. I knew we could work well together.

Signing with Chris and Jim was the best decision I could have made. They're my management but they're also my mates. We've got a WhatsApp group and we communicate really well. They've got me some unbelievable jobs and I've done things I would never have dreamed of.

I was really upfront with them and said that I didn't want my next steps to be all about paid posts on Instagram. Like I said before, it's always been really important to me that my Instagram page is a reflection of my life and not a place to promote stuff I have no interest in.

Paid posts are a surefire way to make a lot of money very quickly, and Chris and Jim could easily have put pressure on me to go down that route. But not once have they ever pushed me to do anything I don't want to. We've had offers of £10K come in and all I have to do is put up a picture of me with a product. But it wouldn't be genuine and I hate that. Jim and Chris care enough about me to not worry about themselves. They take a percentage of what I earn, so they could easily be overloading me with work to make more money, but they put me first.

At one point I had ninety-seven PAs booked in back to back. I did thirty-five of them and then other work got so busy and I got so tired I had to cancel the rest. Chris and Jim could easily have seen the pound signs flashing in front of their eyes and pushed me to do them. They could have worked me until I was completely burnt out but they didn't.

I was so shocked at how much work I already had lined up from day one. I'd been holed up in the villa, but back home the cogs had been turning and deals had been tentatively put in place. It was obvious I wasn't going to be doing a nine-to-five job again any time soon. Not unless I wanted to. At that moment in time everything was way too exciting to even think about it.

· · · · ·

Olivia was having dinner with her parents in the hotel restaurant the same night I had all the management meetings. I was desperate to meet her dad, Kai, for the first time, but whenever I tried to go over and introduce myself someone else would come up and start talking to me. I was literally pushed from pillar to post.

I was so keen to make a good impression on my father-in-law-to-be and I felt so rude. Thankfully that meeting went really well and I got on brilliantly with all of Liv's family. I could talk to her mum about anything. There were times when I'd just call her mum and chat. She was so understanding. My family also loved Liv, so it was like a mutual appreciation society.

By the time I'd spoken to all the management companies it was getting late. Olivia came up to me and said, 'Are you coming over to say hello?' I felt so bad that she had to ask me and I went over straight away.

I got on so well with her dad when we did finally meet, and it's the same with Olivia's whole family. They're such lovely people and they've been so welcoming.

Even though I won't deny that all the attention and new opportunities that were coming my way were exciting, my number one priority was still my relationship with Olivia. We were surrounded by our friends and family for the first time in ages and we were both trying to adjust to life post-*Love Island*.

We didn't know each other at all in the outside world so we kind of had to start again, but the one thing we were 100 per cent certain of was that we wanted to make a proper go of things.

I would hate to go back to that stage now because it felt like we were really distant at times. We were together but it was like we didn't know each other.

We loved spending time alone together, but we were also trying to juggle work commitments so we were all over the place. For the first week it felt strange between us because we were being pulled in so many different directions. We'd fast-tracked our relationship in the villa and then all of a sudden we weren't spending as much time together. We had to reassess things and begin a completely different relationship.

I moved in with Liv in Surrey pretty much straight away but it was obviously very different to being in the villa. It was the first time it had just been the two of us and we began to learn about each other's bad habits. She soon realised how crap I am at cleaning, although I think I've got better recently thanks to living on my own.

We'd seen the real us in the villa because we were both totally ourselves, but there was so much we didn't know about each other. Whenever we had spare time we'd spend it talking and we found out what was important to both of us. Everything changed. We were learning new things every day and after a slightly rocky start back in the real world our relationship went from strength to strength.

It annoyed me when people asked if we were *really* together, as if we were just pretending. We both knew what we had was real and we're both very genuine people, so we would never have been together just because it was what was expected of us. I'm not going to live with someone as a bloody career move. Liv's a diamond and I wanted to be with her more than anything.

Some people started to make me feel like I was doing something wrong by going out with her. Everyone had an opinion about us from watching the show, but no one knew the real Olivia. They knew '*Love Island* Olivia', but they hadn't seen that deeply beneath the surface so they were quick to judge.

I did love Liv in the villa but there wasn't a point where I was *in love* with her. That didn't happen until later on when we started living a proper life together.

Hands down, if I hadn't coupled up with Olivia in *Love Island* I would definitely have come out a single man. All the girls in there were very attractive but Olivia was the only person I felt like I had a proper connection with. I thought she was stunning and she made me laugh, which is so important.

· · · · ·

Olivia and I snatched time together whenever we could, but we barely had time to catch our breath before our schedules were packed with press interviews and photo shoots.

Kem and I were offered our own show, *Straight Outta Love Island*, just two days after we landed back home, so everything was a bit of a whirlwind.

I was pretty much living in a tour van for the few weeks running up to filming. I was going all over the country doing PAs and I was hardly ever at home. Olivia isn't keen on doing PAs and they're much more popular if you're a guy, so she was staying back home at our place. I was getting in at ridiculous times of the morning and going straight to bed. Often I'd drive for two or three hours rather than stay in a hotel, just so I could see Liv.

Olivia was really understanding and she knew I had to do the PAs if I wanted to make money, but we didn't get any time to do nice things together. We wanted to do really simple things like go out for dinner or go to the cinema, but the timings were always off. If she was working I wouldn't be, and vice versa. I was worried it would have a negative effect on us but I knew we'd get through it.

· · · · ·

I quickly learned my lesson when it came to drinking on PAs. All my mates came to the first five or so I did, and it was proper party time. I hadn't seen them properly for ages because of *Love Island*, so it was the perfect excuse for us to get together and have a few drinks. I lived it up and had a wicked time, but when you're doing eight or nine of those a week you soon run out of steam.

Once my mates stopped coming with me there was no point

in me drinking on those nights. If I was just me and my tour manager, Dan, I didn't need to drink. My job was to do meet and greets and chat with people, and I enjoyed that whether I was drunk or sober.

I still do PAs sometimes now and if I get a bit of a run of them I can spend hours and hours on the tour bus, which is basically a giant Mercedes. It's got six seats in the back, so I can put my feet up and lie down, but annoyingly I find it really hard to sleep in it.

Dan is brilliant because he can tell when I want to chat and when I don't. I can't stand it when I get into a taxi when I'm really tired and the driver wants to talk for the entire journey. Dan knows if I'm tired and I just want to chill out and he would never take offence at that.

· · · · ·

When Kem and I first started filming the show I was still doing a lot of PAs. I'd go to clubs and do my bit, get in at three or four in the morning, and then a taxi would be outside waiting to take me to filming at 6 a.m.

We filmed in a pub on the very first day and Kem and I were both so knackered we had to have a nap while the camera crew stood around waiting for us. I felt terrible and really diva-ish, but I couldn't keep my eyes open. After four nights of barely any sleep at all I was a wreck. Kem was on a similar schedule, so the pair of us were really struggling.

I did three PAs in one night once, in Liverpool, Chester and Bolton, and I stayed in Essex that night. I got back to the house at 7.45 a.m. and I had to be at V Festival to do some filming for the show at 10 a.m. I had about half an hour to sleep before I had to have a shower and put on some clean clothes. Sometimes it's worse if you have a bit of sleep instead of none at all, and I probably should have powered on through. I felt awful. That's probably the most tired I've ever felt in my life.

We still had a great day though and we met loads of people like Louisa Johnson, Clean Bandit, and we finally got to properly meet Stormzy and Youngun. We were by the side of the stage when Stormzy performed and he gave us a shout-out in front of tens of thousands of people. How mad is that?

As time went on I got more and more run down and it got to the point where Mike, the series producer of *Straight Outta Love Island*, sat Kem and me down and said, 'This isn't okay, you're going to have to start cancelling PAs. You're turning up too tired to film. How are you supposed to be enthusiastic about anything when you're exhausted all the time?'

He was totally right. It was something we already knew but I guess we just needed someone to say it. After that I cancelled around sixty PAs. I hated letting people down but it was one of those situations where it was impossible to keep everyone happy. We owed it to ITV to be on form and there were times when I had to have a quick lie-down just so I could film a scene without yawning all the way through. I couldn't physically do everything that was in my diary. Something had to give and I had to put the show first.

It was a shame because I actually really enjoyed doing the PAs. All the people I met were lovely. I know some people have had a bit of trouble on PAs, with guys trying to start fights with them or girls coming on to them, but I had a great time. Don't get me wrong, some of the nights were carnage – what do you expect when you're going to a club full of drunken people? – but 99 per cent of the time they were still really well organised.

A girl fainted on the first PA I ever did in Blackpool, and I hoped it wasn't a sign of things to come. But worse was around the corner. When I was in Southampton quite early on I was onstage and everyone surged forward to see me. One girl got crushed and she was rushed to hospital, where they discovered she'd broken her leg. I felt absolutely terrible about it.

I remember going to another PA in Guildford and when I drove past an hour beforehand the queues were ridiculous. Apparently they had to turn 1,000 people away. I went onstage at 12.30 a.m. and I could tell that the club was too full. People down the front were getting crushed and it didn't feel safe. After five minutes I got pulled offstage by the club's management because they said it was dangerous for me to be there. I didn't want to let people down so I said I'd wait for a bit to see if things calmed down.

While I was waiting at the back of the club I walked past a room and saw a girl lying down on a bed crying her eyes out. It turned out she'd been pushed over and hurt herself and I felt awful.

I went in to see if she was okay, but that was a very clear warning sign that it wasn't safe for me to go back out. In the end I had no choice but to call it a night and head home.

I always try to stay longer than I need to on PAs, and the only time I actually leave on time is if I've got more than one to do in a night. I once did a PA in Leeds followed by another one in Wakefield, and I ended up going back to the Leeds one again afterwards because I didn't feel like I'd spent enough time with everyone.

Girls can be pretty blatant and lay it on me when they meet me on those nights. I had people coming up to me and asking why I'm with Olivia and then bare flirting with me, which I find really rude. You would never walk up to a stranger in a club and ask why they were with their girlfriend or boyfriend, but because I'm in the public eye it seems to be an okay thing to say. I still get upset if people say hurtful things about Liv. I get much more upset when they say things about her than I do when they say things about me.

I used to react but now I don't. If I do it opens the door for people to get even nastier so it's not worth it. The best thing to do is ignore them. I've learned to control my temper more now. Interacting with people on social media just makes things a hundred times worse. Instead of putting people in their place they come back at you even harder because they know they've got a reaction. It's just not worth it.

I've been given some really sweet presents on PAs. I get a lot of cashew nuts and I've had a few cuddly polar bears. One girl even framed a really nice picture of Olivia and me and gave it to me.

The *Love Island* tattoos are always a bit of a shock though. A girl had my name tattooed on the inside of her arm, and another one had 'Little Bit Leave It' written on her hip.

· · · · ·

Amazingly, Kem and I got to go to America to shoot some scenes for *Straight Outta Love Island*. It was my first time in the US and we flew to LA and did all the touristy stuff, like going to see the Hollywood sign and the Walk of Fame. We also went to Compton, which is considered to be the home of hip hop, and it was unreal.

Kem and I were driving around LA one day and we looked at each other and said, 'How the hell are we filming our own show? What even *is* this?' It was something you could only dream about, but it was actually happening.

It was a brilliant experience but of course that took me away from Olivia again. She was involved in some of the filming on the show, so at least we got to spend time with each other then, but there were also big chunks when it was just Kem and me dicking about, so instead Liv and I spoke on the phone continually.

• • • • •

Next on the agenda was the release of mine and Kem's debut single. We knew just after we left *Love Island* that Sony's label Relentless wanted to put a single out with us, and of course when *Straight Outta Love Island* came along it was a great way to showcase the journey in the lead-up to the release date.

We worked evenings in the studio recording the single. Loads of people from the record label came along, as well as the other people who were involved, like Zdot, Splurgeboys, Trey, Pro Green, Youngun . . . It was wicked.

We were asked to headline our own gig at Ministry of Sound and it sold out straight away. We performed our single for the first time that night and even though no one knew the single, everyone was singing along. There was a mosh pit and everything. I felt well rock 'n' roll.

We shot our music video in a massive house in London and I was buzzing about it. But annoyingly it was one of those days where a serious lack of sleep crept up on me and I looked like shit. I knew I did because a member of the crew suggested that I have a sleep while they were setting up the camera equipment. That's never a great sign.

I found a cinema room at the bottom of the house and I

went and slept in there for a full two hours. If they'd told me I had to pay £5,000 for that sleep I would have paid it, and then some.

I initially felt worse when I woke up, but within half an hour I pulled some energy back and I was good to go. A bit of make-up helped make my tired eyes look a bit more with it and the day ended up going really well. There was a really good vibe and the energy of all the people who appeared in the video kept me going.

I still kept getting waves of exhaustion but even if I was on my last legs I knew I had to pull it out of the bag because it wasn't just me I was letting down, it was everyone who was working on the video. Whether it's the film crew, the hair and make-up artists or the catering people, there is always someone you're going to make life a bit more difficult for.

That was the main thing that gave me a kick up the arse on the days I really wanted to stay in bed. I am quite lazy, but the thought of other people going out of their way for me made me get up, get dressed and get in the taxi.

I never go on a night out if I have to be somewhere the following morning these days. I just can't do it. Even if I was invited somewhere sick I wouldn't do that to myself. I need my sleep badly and I know I would suffer all the next day.

I've got into a more sensible routine now. If you can call it a routine because there is no such thing in this business. If I've got a big work day I'll try to get to bed as early as possible. I've learned the hard way that it's no fun filming for twelve hours on two hours' sleep.

I really appreciate my sleep now, more than ever.

I thought I'd kind of adapted to having so little sleep around that time, and it's only now looking back that I realise I was constantly spaced out. Sometimes I'd be having conversations with people and I'd start to think 'Am I making sense?' It was quite scary.

When I did get a decent night's sleep – I'm talking six or seven hours here, which felt like a real luxury – I felt really odd the following day because I was so used to existing on coffee and adrenalin.

I don't think my body knew whether it was coming or going. You can only keep going at that pace for so long before your body and mind start to suffer. I get moody and miserable and quiet, but thankfully it doesn't tend to kick off my anxiety so that's one plus. But I do really keep an eye on that kind of thing and try to look after myself.

I am a pretty good sleeper but I do weird things sometimes. I used to sleepwalk a bit when I was a kid, and after we filmed *Straight Outta Love Island* I started having weird dreams that people had put cameras in mine and Olivia's bedroom, or they were coming in and taking photos of me.

I'd yell in my sleep and tell people to get out of the room and leave me alone. It used to wake Olivia up and it really freaked her out. I only had a small break in between *Love Island* finishing and starting work on *Straight Outta Love Island*, so for a very long time most of my life was captured on camera. I guess that ended up having quite a big effect on me.

There were definitely times when I wanted to take a step back from everything and just have quiet times, but I didn't ever regret making the decision to pursue an entertainment career. At the end of the day I'd made my choice and I had to stick with it.

Was it weird being filmed all the time? Yes. Did I have days where I wanted to run back to the Cotswolds and hide under a duvet? Yes. Did I ever wish I'd turned my back on the opportunities I've been given after *Love Island* and gone back to my old job? Absolutely not. I try to be as professional as I can be and crack on, even when things are tricky.

• • • • •

The dreams carried on for about two months and sometimes one of them would last for so long Olivia would have to wake me up. Because I was having a lot of broken sleep that also made me feel tired, and it was horrible waking up worrying about what I'd done in my sleep. I even kicked Liv one night. God knows what I was dreaming about but she wasn't that happy about it.

I sleepwalked a bit while I was on *Love Island*. I got up and opened the drawers underneath my bed because I was looking for salt. It was all caught on camera, and I also said to Kem and Amber, 'Hey, did I dream it? Did someone come in and put salt in all our hands?' Amber said no and I replied, 'I've dreamed that, haven't I?' They started laughing and I went back to sleep. I only know that because I've watched the clip back since. I didn't remember a thing about it at the time.

Dreams are so weird because you can have a quick thought during the day and then forget about it, but that then turns into a really mad dream that night. It just shows how powerful your mind is. I don't think dreams are things you hope will happen; they're just a collection of random thoughts.

• • • • •

Kem and I were really looking forward to 'Little Bit Leave It' being released, and were buzzing in the lead-up. The whole experience was brilliant, but if we could change anything about that time we'd go back and rethink the release date.

The last episode of *Straight Outta Love Island* aired on a Monday night so it was decided that the single should come out the same evening. Songs are usually released on a Friday so they have a full week of sales before their chart position is announced, but we only had three full days to tally up sales. Despite that we still went in at number 15. At that point it was the highest charting first week entry of 2017 by any artist, which is mad. Imagine if we'd had a full week of sales. I reckon the single would have gone top ten, and maybe even top five.

Despite what was written in the papers there was no fallout with Marcel over the single. He tweeted saying: 'Boys, the tune sounds sick!!! I hope u did the right thing with the chorus & bars I wrote.' But it wasn't written to piss us off and he was quite upset about the way it was taken out of context. I had a chat with him about it and he was totally fine. We're good mates with him and always will be.

As for mine and Kem's musical future? We're both too busy to do anything else at the moment but that's not to say we won't make more music together in the future. It's on hold for now but watch this space.

The things I would
save first in a fire

I'd grab Cash first because he'd melt otherwise.

I've got three polar bear ornaments – a daddy and two little kids – so I'd take those.

I've got a polar bear teddy too, so he would come.

I'd have to grab my watches. I wouldn't want to lose them.

My phone. It would probably be on charge somewhere so I'd have to find it first.

I'd take some underwear so I had some fresh ones to put on the next day.

I'd also carry out the photo frames with pictures in. They're sentimental, aren't they?

My silver rings. I've got quite into rings recently.

A pair of socks so I can keep warm. I wouldn't need a dressing gown because the fire brigade would give me one of those sheets of foil when they arrived.

8

Cheap Shot

I got thrown into the centre of the celeb world very quickly. Even though my management told me a bit about what I could expect, nothing could have prepared me for how mad things were. I felt like I was on a train that was going 500 miles an hour, and it wasn't about to go into reverse any time soon. But I loved it. It was a total whirlwind and I did a lot of learning. Espccially when it came to press intrusion.

It's no secret that paps go to some pretty extreme lengths to get photos. Otherwise how would they get all the photos you see in the press? But I never thought for a minute they would be so interested in me and Olivia they'd sleep in a van outside our flat. Seriously, *that's* what happened.

Olivia and I would wake up some mornings and we'd see photos in the papers that had been taken of us the day or night before, and we'd had no idea they'd been there. A lot of them were in the grounds around our place so it was shocking.

The flat where we first lived together was on a complex on private property, so it was illegal for the paps to be on the land. That didn't stop them though. They were doing stakeouts in the car park and using long lenses to snap us when we came in and out of the building. It genuinely felt like we were being stalked and it was scary. You're supposed to feel safe in your own home and we really didn't.

We don't know how they found out where we were living, but Olivia is pretty sure some guys on motorbikes followed her home from an event in London one night. There were pictures of her and her friend going through our front door on several websites the following day, and they were wearing the same clothes they had on the previous evening. Once one pap knows where you live, the chances are it won't be long before others find out.

Some of the photos were so boring. They were literally of me walking to a taxi, or Olivia coming back from the hairdresser. However, the press managed to make them more interesting by writing inaccurate stories to run alongside them. There was a photo of me that was taken as I was walking outside our apartment that was captioned 'Chris goes to visit Olivia'. How could I be visiting her when I lived with her?

Around the same time, weird things started happening that we can only put down to the press. . .

Several pairs of my trainers went missing from the boot room outside our flat. I was working at an event when Olivia phoned me and said: 'I've just found a pair of your trainers tied to the railings outside.' What the fuck? When I got home and saw them it was obvious they'd been put there for a reason. It was a pretty open area, and if I'd taken them down photographers would have been able to get a really clear shot of me.

I saw some other pap shots of me that were taken the same

day, so photographers must have been lying in wait. But why would you want pictures of me untying some trainers from railings? What kind of story were they going to write to go with that? It was insane.

It was awful to know these people had been outside our front door, especially when Liv was on her own. She popped out to the shop one morning and got papped holding her phone. It said 'OJ Hughes' on the cover on the back, which was only a bit of fun, but within hours there was a story online asking whether we'd got engaged.

It was all getting out of control so both mine and Olivia's management complained, but the website that was running the shots claimed that the pictures were taken from a footpath near our place, so it was totally legal. The nearest footpath to us is quite far away, and I'm not being funny but even with zoom lenses you'd have to be pretty close to someone to get such a clear shot of a phone case.

Later the same day Olivia went to put something in our boot room, which is also where we keep our rubbish, and she realised some full bin bags had been stolen. She'd only been out for twenty minutes that morning, but during that time someone had come into the building and walked out with several black bags full of crap. They probably went through it trying to find a story.

I reckon they were hoping to find a pregnancy test because there had been some rumours that Olivia was expecting. We'd put up some pictures of us together at Ascot the week before and it wasn't a great angle so some people on Instagram started questioning whether Liv was pregnant. She'd probably had a couple of proseccos or was feeling a bit bloated that day, but the papers were looking for answers.

Of course we can't say 100 per cent that it was paps that did those things, but no kids lived on our estate and our neighbours were all proper grown-ups who wouldn't spend their time nicking strangers' shoes and rubbish. We couldn't wait to move in the end because we wanted to put a stop to all that. Our new place had high walls and coded gates so it's pretty impossible for people to get pictures of us in there.

• • • • •

In the early days Olivia and I used to spend a lot of time tweeting about untrue stories. But we started to let it go because the people behind it didn't deserve that level of attention and the traffic to their sites. That's probably why they're doing it. They'd much rather have that reaction rather than us say nothing, so it draws attention to the story, but we got wise to it now. At the end of the day we knew what's true and what's not.

Set-up pap shots are the norm for people these days and I'm not saying for a minute that we didn't let photographers know if we're going to a nice event or something so they could come along and take photos of us for the press to use. You'd be hard pushed to find a celebrity who doesn't do that. But it's a very different thing when someone is hanging around outside your home taking sneaky shots of private moments.

I'm very aware that Olivia and I both play the game and we know how the industry works now, but I still find press intrusion pretty disgusting at times. We even had to contact a solicitor on occasion because things have got so bad. Yes, we're in the public eye, but does that mean we're not allowed to have a bit of privacy and to feel safe?

I'm not moaning about attention on the whole. I'm not stupid and I know I'm going to be recognised most times I go out, and that's part and parcel of what I do. People who stop me in the street feel like they know me and I wouldn't be doing what I do if it wasn't for them.

There are times when I want to go out and have a bit of normality, like when Liv and I pop out for breakfast at a local café in our onesies. Last time we went we didn't even get a chance to order our food and there was a bit of a queue for selfies. But we were happy to do them.

Shopping centres are the worst. I went to the Trafford Centre in Manchester and I was taking selfies for about two hours. Once someone clocks that you're there everyone soon catches on. I always do as much as I can. At the end of the day, I'm where I am because of those people and I'm so bloody grateful.

I've been asked for selfies in the maddest places, like service stations or toilets. A car once stopped on a main road and two lads jumped out and asked to have a picture with me. They were holding up the traffic and loads of cars were beeping their horns at them but they didn't care. Olivia and I were also in Five Guys and I was biting into my burger when someone came up and snapped a photo when I had ketchup dripping down my chin.

Some people are really respectful, but several people have said things to me like: 'I know you don't want to take a picture with me but you're going to. This is the price you pay for being famous.' I was really tired one day so I was leaning against a wall in Costa Coffee with my eyes closed and I saw the flash of a camera phone. When I opened my eyes a girl was taking a picture of me. She laughed and walked off and I stood there thinking 'Did that just happen?'

Like everyone, I have days when I'm not feeling my best, and when people shout at me in the street I just ignore them. I feel really rude but when it's the fiftieth person to shout something I just don't have it in me to reply.

I've never had anyone being aggressive towards me but I can imagine it happens. You see it all the time. Someone becomes a bit of a villain because of what's said about them in the papers and the public turns against them without knowing the facts and they can get a lot of hassle. I guess I'm just me though, and I try to live a chilled life. I'm not a show-off and I don't go out begging for attention.

• • • • •

For a long time I was worried about going out looking a mess in case I got papped. I always thought I had to look a certain way. I saw some photos online of Declan Donnelly shopping and the journalist had written a story about him looking a mess. He tweeted something like 'sorry I don't dress up to go to the supermarket. I'll make sure my hair and make-up is done next time'. I totally get that.

People make you feel like you can't be seen unless you're looking your absolute best, which is ridiculous. I don't sit around my flat with my hair done and a nice outfit on. If I've got a day off I'll be in a onesie and my hair will be all over the place. If I happen to go out at some point looking like that, so be it. You can't be precious about that kind of thing because it will do your head in. I'm only human at the end of the day, and sometimes I look a bit shit. That's just the way it is.

I haven't changed who I am at all and I'm happy being quiet and sitting in on my own watching TV. I mainly watch sport but I love films like *Pretty Woman*, *Dumb and Dumber* and the original *Point Break*. I can watch them over and over again. I've seen *Shooter* with Mark Wahlberg about ten times now. I'm one of those people that doesn't like watching new films. I like watching old ones I know I like over and over again. I like to stick with what I know.

• • • • •

I don't feel the need to run around trying to get papped all the time. Staying in the press isn't my prime motivation in life. I also don't feel the need to tell everyone every little thing I'm doing. Of course I'm on social media but I'm not Instagramming a photo every time I eat or letting people know I'm off to buy new socks. I'd rather *eat* my dinner than take a photo of it.

Some people enjoy sharing everything with the public, and fair play to them, but it doesn't bother me that people don't have an insight into every little bit of my life. How can you maintain any kind of normality if they do? And before you say 'Hang on, he's written a book,' that's because I want to put my honest story out there so I don't keep getting asked about things that aren't true.

I would hate it if I'd become well known and got lost in showbiz. I still manage to have a life away from photo shoots or signings. I went to Tesco the other day wearing a tracksuit with my hood up and I must have looked like a bit of a chav. It's not that I think I'm big time and didn't want people to see me, but I don't court attention every time I walk out of the house. I don't need people to recognise me or ask for photos in order to feel good about myself.

I don't get nervous about going to red carpet events and

having my photo taken any more either. I sometimes prefer doing the red carpet to going to the actual events. I usually walk it with a chaperone or one of my managers, so I feel like I've got someone on my side if anyone throws a really tricky question at me.

There have been times when a member of the press has started chatting away to me asking me really fun questions, and then they'll suddenly lay some really hard-core one on me about a story that's been in the press that week. I feel bad because I know that people who work on magazines and newspapers have been sent along with strict instructions from their editor to get the answers they want, but there are some things you don't want to discuss when you're surrounded by hundreds of cameras and members of the public.

I like going to events and meeting new people, and everyone has been massively supportive, especially other reality stars. We're all in the same boat at the end of the day, and we get what each other is going through. Reality TV is so massive now and all of the people involved in it basically go from living their normal lives one day to being tabloid fodder the next, so it's nice to chat to people who have experienced the same things you have.

• • • • •

I'm still shocked about the amount of free stuff I get given. I can stay in some hotels free of charge, and I get sent all kinds of things because companies want me to wear their clothes or eat their food. I do get it but I'm not someone who needs a lot. It would make more sense if they gave free gifts to people who really need it. I'm not going to make out that I turn

This is me with a retired Grand National winner called Earth Summit, who I occasionally rode out when I was younger.

Doing some jumps with Rita. I was fearless around horses from a young age.

With the rest of my class at school. I'm the one at the front
in the grey shirt with the amazing hair.

Playing for Swindon Centre of Excellence. I even had a dodgy footballer's haircut.

With my amazing mum, who is always the person I turn to in a crisis.

This was taken at my brother Tom's wedding. All the men in the photo are my brothers or cousins.

My mates and me hanging out at the cricket at Edgbaston. We definitely had a few beers that day.

Going for a ride with my friends Richie and Aidan.

This was the first time Olivia visited the farm and I introduced
her to some of my best mates – the cows.

This is one of my favourite pictures of Olivia and me. It makes me feel happy and sad at the same time.

Cash looks well handsome in this picture. That little chap means the world to me.

Hanging out backstage at V Festival with Krept and Konan.
That's probably the coolest I've ever felt.

away packages when they arrive because I don't, but the way it works is a bit messed up, isn't it? I end up giving quite a lot away.

I've stayed in some really nice hotels, like Malmaison, and they always offer me an hour's free massage each day. And I can go into a Topman store and choose any clothes I like. Sometimes my flat is such a mess because it's full of freebies.

I could get a lot more free stuff than I already do but I honestly don't need it. For instance, when Olivia asked me what I wanted for Christmas last year I didn't know what to say because there was nothing I needed, which has never, ever happened to me before.

· · · · ·

I genuinely had no idea what to expect from fame. I know this is a ridiculous thing to admit but I didn't used to watch a lot of reality TV before *Love Island*. Olivia's got me into a few different programmes now but I was a bit clueless before. I can't wait to watch the next *Love Island* though. It will feel so strange watching it knowing I've lived it.

I think there will be so much expectation next time around. There wasn't any when we went on the show because it had done well in previous years, but nothing like when we were in there.

I do wonder if the people who are picked to go in it this year will feel a lot of pressure. I hope they're not too aware of what's going on because people are best when they're just being themselves. That why our series worked so well, I guess. None of us really had a clue what we were doing, and for all we knew just five people could have been watching. No one was trying to be someone they're not.

I did used to watch *TOWIE* a little bit when it first started and I used to think 'How are these guys driving round in these nice cars? What do they do to make money?' I didn't get it. I didn't know what managers were for and what they did for you. I didn't even know what a PA was. I knew absolutely nothing. When I got management and started doing work outside of *Love Island* I began to get my head around why some reality stars are rich.

It's honestly ridiculous what you can get paid for. I mean, the fees you get for wearing a brand's clothing to an event where you're going to be papped is crazy. You get holidays, VIP discounts for cars and free meals. I would expect a sportsperson or a musician to get all that kind of stuff, but a reality star? That's been a huge shock to me.

I'm mates with Gaz from *Geordie Shore* and he told me recently that he'd just done his thousandth PA. Imagine doing a thousand PAs? I only got to thirty-five. The money people make from PAs is incredible, and fair play to them. Gaz does work bloody hard.

If I'm being honest I did think fame would be a breeze. I thought it would be non-stop fun and going out to parties and meeting cool people. And yes, there is that side to it, and that's great, but there's so much you don't think about.

I went on *Love Island* thinking I would do the show and then go back to my regular life. I know some people went on hoping to go into TV presenting or something afterwards, but I hadn't thought that far ahead. No one had any idea the show would end up being as big as it was.

I remember the producers saying to me that they'd be happy if it was as popular as it had been the previous year, but I think our season outdid all expectations, and then some.

I often think people are interested in me because I'm with Olivia and they're invested in us as a couple. It's really nice, and we have super-fans who we know, who will tweet ten times a day about us and make amazing professional-looking edited videos of what we've been up to.

One of them, Sophie, came and saw me when I did a Topman meet and greet in Manchester last year and she brought along this photo album filled with pictures of Olivia and me. She'd put so much effort into it and it means so much when people support us.

I am very grounded and I'm aware I'm not Harry Styles or Jay-Z. That level of fame would do my head in. I wouldn't like it if I was unable to go out and do normal, everyday things. I may get recognised doing them these days but I can still go about my business most of the time.

· · · · ·

It's weird going from living on a farm in the countryside to the life I'm living now in such a short space of time. My life used to be pretty quiet, and now it feels like everything is on fast forward. I'm getting used to it but it's a really big change and I have to balance it out by going back to the Cotswolds a lot and being 'normal', if that makes sense. I go back regularly because it feels really important to me. It keeps me really grounded. The cows and pigs don't give a shit that I'm famous. It will always be home to me, and it will always be the place I go to when things get too much.

When work gets crazily busy I don't always have time to see the people I love as much as I want to. For a while Mum started to keep up with what was happening in my life by reading magazine interviews I'd done. She said she only knew

I was going home for Christmas last year because she read it in *OK!* magazine, and that made me feel really bad. That was a bit of a wake-up call actually. It made me realise I hadn't been speaking to my family as much as I should so I phone them regularly now. Mum and I talk on the phone a lot.

Mum is pleased that I'm getting to do something I enjoy every day, and that I'm making my own money and I don't ask for handouts any more. She's very supportive but her and my dad don't read anything about me online, so she doesn't have to worry about the gossip stories, which is a good thing.

They had some paps up at the farm just after *Love Island*. They were asking all sorts of questions about me, and also mine and Olivia's relationship, but that's all stopped now. The paps probably realised they'd have a tough job getting anything out of my mum and dad.

• • • • •

One of the major perks of becoming well known is being invited onto the kind of TV shows I've always watched and loved. Kem and I got invited to appear on *Celebrity Juice* and that's such a big show to do.

I didn't realise that you get properly boozed while you're on there. I was drinking gin and lemonade so I was quite drunk by the end of filming. No wonder people agree to do such mad things on there. Kem and I had to lick chocolate off the tops of éclairs that were attached to each other's crotches. Standard.

I also got asked to take part in *Celebrity Ghost Hunt Live* last September, which was hosted by Rylan Clark-Neal. I appeared on the show with Charlotte Crosby and her boyfriend at the time, Stephen Bear, as well as Charlotte Dawson and

Ampika Pickston from *Real Housewives of Cheshire*. We filmed it at this 200-year-old house in Essex called Harwich Redoubt Fort, which is supposed to be one of the most haunted buildings in the country.

The whole experience was freaky. I got voted to go into one of the rooms on my own where they used this really advanced sound sensor technology. There was this box in the middle of the room that draws in energy and I got given a boy's name by, like, the actual box. I know that sounds mad but I heard it come out of it really clearly. Only I can't remember what the name was now, which is annoying.

I could also hear someone or something scratching the wall behind me, like someone had started picking at the wall with their fingernail. I was so scared I was frozen to the spot, and even though I wanted to I couldn't bring myself to look round to where the noise was coming from. It was as clear as day and I wish other people had been in that room with me and felt what I felt because it's hard to get across how fucking weird it was.

I'd never had an experience like that before but my brothers Will and James are both adamant they saw ghosts in their rooms when they were younger. They believe in them completely.

A lot of people who haven't seen ghosts don't believe in them and I totally understand why, but I've heard too many stories and experienced too many things for there to not be something in it. It's fascinating. It's not like people ever get hurt or killed by ghosts or spirits, but it still freaks me out a bit.

We all did a séance with a Ouija board round a table in one of the rooms and my arms became paralysed. I could *not* lift my arms off the table no matter how hard I tried. It was like my forearms were made of lead and my whole body was burning. I'd been freezing cold the entire day, and then when we sat down at that table my whole body heated up. Everyone else was feeling the same and it made no sense at all because there was no heating in there.

We all had our fingers on the planchette (the little wooden thing that moves) on the Ouija board and I swear to God it was moving without anyone pushing it. There's no way one single person could have been pushing it in all those different directions from where they were sitting. The board spelt out Bear's granddad's name and he was well freaked out. It was definitely moving of its own accord and that was unbelievably unnerving. There was no denying there was an unexplainable energy in that room.

• • • • •

For a few weeks after filming I genuinely believed I was possessed. Olivia did too. My sleepwalking got worse than ever and it was like I turned into someone else. I started to sit up in bed screaming three or four times a night and Liv had to wake me up by shaking me really hard.

I also became convinced someone was trying to get in through our front door. One night I got out of bed and stood and stared at the door for ages, and then suddenly I came to and wondered what the hell I was doing.

Things were so bad we had to cancel a photo shoot because my nightmares had been so bad the previous night. I had barely slept a wink and Olivia was so exhausted she ended up going and sleeping on the sofa. I don't reckon I'll be going ghost hunting again any time soon.

I do still have mad dreams and talk or shout in my sleep

now but the sleepwalking has calmed right down. I'm not sure if it's anything that will go away completely but at least it's more under control now.

• • • • •

There was a rumour last year that Kem and I were going to go on *Big Brother* and *I'm a Celebrity . . .*, and if I had to choose between the two of them I would probably go for *I'm a Celebrity . . .* because I know more about it. I've never actually watched an episode of *Big Brother* so I don't really know what goes on. They're all in a house, aren't they? It sounds a bit like *Love Island*, but without constant sun and relationship rows.

I'm genuinely terrified of all the things they have in the jungle, like rats and snakes, but I would be up for giving it a go. I would have to have some kind of phobia counselling before I went in. I think I'd have health issues otherwise.

I love watching the show and I find it fascinating and the people on it are so brave.

• • • • •

I know a lot of people think that when you go on a reality show you instantly share this unbreakable bond with everyone you meet on there. I'm sorry to burst the *Love Island* bubble but we're not all best mates now. We don't have a WhatsApp group and we don't meet up for big nights out. In fact, we don't meet up at all. I don't see anyone from *Love Island* apart from Kem. We'll always be mates.

There haven't been any fallouts and if we bump into each other at events we'll have a nice catch-up, but we're not planning group holidays or lavish reunions. They're getting on with their stuff and I'm doing my own thing. Simple as that. I've got a lot of time and respect for them but we're all getting on with our own lives. It was amazing at the time but I suppose we've all moved on.

Word association

Mug – Mike

Watch – Rolex

Blanket – Bed

Dog – Dachshund

Snow – Christmas

Rubber – Condom

Pen – Biro

Duvet – Sleep

Sandwich – Coronation chicken

Light – Camera

Moon – Night-time

Wings – Eagle

Plant – Daffodil

Water – Voss

Walk – Countryside

Body – Willy

Cat – Itchy. I like them but they make me itch

Drink – Peroni

Farm – Cow

Crisps – Paprika

9

The Price of Fame

I have to say, aside from intrusive paps, I was really lucky with the press when I came out of *Love Island*. They were all really supportive. That is until the whole Katie Price saga happened. That was a game changer for me.

Much has been said – too much in fact – about it all and I don't want to give what was just a very silly story any more time by going into the ins and outs of how it all came about. I know what happened and I can sleep easily knowing that I did no wrong. What I would love to be able to change, though, is the way in which I reacted when things blew up.

I learned a lot of lessons during the weeks and months of stories appearing about myself and Katie Price. Even though it was all a load of crap it did become a pivotal moment, particularly when it came to the press. I soon discovered that things in this world don't run in the way they do in the world I had come from. Before I became well-known, if someone said something about me that wasn't true or was misleading,

I would call them out on it – and anyone else who happened to join in. Yet in this situation, speaking up for myself and pointing out things I knew weren't true only caused more scrutiny and it felt like people were desperate to catch me out.

• • • • •

I always told Olivia when other girls send me flirty messages because I want to be totally upfront with her. I find it weird that people didn't respect the fact I had a girlfriend but some clearly don't, but Liv and I were 100 per cent honest with each other about things like that. Olivia got sent messages from random guys too, and it stopped us worrying if we both know exactly what was going on.

Even though I felt comfortable that she knew all about what had happened and how I had played no part, I couldn't just leave it at that. I wanted everyone to know I'd done no wrong so I posted something online. I wish I hadn't now as I instantly felt that anxiety rearing its head all over again.

• • • • •

The day I was shooting my L'Eau de Chris campaign for Topman my management were still getting calls. This thing wasn't going to go away. I shot that campaign with Rankin, who is an incredible photographer, and I was so honoured to work with him. I had really good people around so I should have enjoyed that day. Instead I was worried about what was going to happen next. It's ironic that I was shooting a campaign about mental health and anxiety and there was this great big issue in the background causing me no end of stress.

I wanted to concentrate on the most important thing, which was the shoot, but it was hard for me to stick my head in the sand when people were saying that I was lying about what had really gone on just so I could try to stay relevant. I'm not that desperate for a headline.

The worst thing I ever did was rise to the goading and show I was bothered.

• • • • •

It was such hard work dealing with all of that when I was so new to the industry. People think I have it so easy but I can't explain what it's like living in an environment where people are obsessed with taking you down. On the one hand public interest is the reason that I am able to do the job I do, but sometimes what comes with it is not fun.

I've had to grow another layer of skin to protect myself, and I've had to get my hot-headedness under control. It got me into trouble on sports fields when I was younger, and now I'm in the public eye it's got me into trouble for altogether different reasons. I've always been quick to react and once I see red I really see red. But I'm learning each day. For a very long time, I didn't have a PR representative to act on my behalf, so when shit happened I dealt with it myself, which I should *not* do.

Olivia is a very strong person but she's also very emotional like me, so I was worried about the effect all the negative press would have on her. I wanted Olivia to have total peace of mind so I sent my Snapchat username and password to her manager, Scarlett, and I let her log on, look through my entire history and print off whatever she wanted so she could see what had been sent to who. That meant Liv knew 100 per cent that I was telling the truth.

• • • • •

I would like to set the record straight about the fact that Olivia did not lose weight over the stress of the Katie Price situation, as was reported in the press. She did lose weight because she'd been rushing around so much, but it was nothing to do with what had been going on.

Olivia was being trolled a lot online and people were saying she was too skinny and needed to eat a few burgers, so she addressed the comments in her column in *New!* magazine. She admitted she'd lost weight because she'd been working a lot and things had been stressing her out, but the press twisted her words and said that it was down to the anxiety of the Katie saga. That's so not true. Olivia wouldn't lose a second's sleep over it.

Something else that really upset me about the stupid drama with Katie Price was that it threatened to affect my relationship with Rylan. I'd always got on really well with him and when we did *Celebrity Ghost Hunt Live* together we had a brilliant time. I think he's a great guy and I've got a lot of respect for him.

Obviously Rylan does the showbiz section on *This Morning* so he has to address topics that are in the news, and it would have been weird if he hadn't addressed it when it was all over the press. But when he did, it meant the story was all over the papers *again* so I was annoyed. I consider him to be a friend, which is why the situation was so annoying and hurtful.

The following night both Rylan and I were invited to the Specsavers awards and I was still angry that he'd opened up the wound again. It was clear he wanted to chat and clear the air but when he approached me on the red carpet I wasn't in the mood.

There wasn't any big bust-up, honestly. I just told him I

didn't want to talk to him. He said he didn't understand what he'd done wrong and that I was being ridiculous. I said something like 'We'll talk about it later.'

We were in each other's faces and yes, it was awkward, but it wasn't like we were about to start throwing punches. It was just a heated discussion and it was made out to be a lot more than it was. I told him to get out of my face, and as I did his manager put her hand on his shoulder to get his attention. All the paps took photos of that moment and the press claimed that she was holding him back from attacking me, which was crap.

Once I got inside the venue loads of journalists came up and asked what was going on. I remained tight-lipped because I didn't want it to become a big thing. I did not need any more shit being written about me.

Rylan was presenting the show that night and during a break his manager came over to me and said he wanted to have a chat to me. I owed it to Rylan to hear him out and listen to what he had to say.

We went to a dingy corner where no one could see us and he said to me: 'Look, I see a bit of me in you when I was starting out. I was responding to people and biting back at things I knew were bollocks and that was the worst thing I could have done. I had death threats and all sorts but five years later I've learned from it. I'm not saying you're in the wrong for feeling frustrated because I get it, but you should be enjoying this time. The campaign you've done for Topman is unbelievable and you should be able to appreciate it.' Then he laughed and said, 'You're the first person who's ignored me the whole time I've been in this industry. But what you don't realise is that there are already three articles about our "bust-up" online.'

We made a decision to squash the fight rumours straight away by messaging each other on Twitter, which we did.

I watched Rylan's interview on *This Morning* the next day and he talked about our 'fight' and made a joke of it, but that didn't stop the press having a field day. No one actually knew what really happened between us that night but people were writing stories about it like it was the fallout of the century.

. . . . .

Olivia and I stopped talking about Message-gate altogether because we knew if we mentioned it we'd only add fuel to a fire that we were sick of seeing burn unnecessarily. Other people still brought it up all the time but as far as we were concerned it was over.

Amidst it all, though, Olivia put a really lovely message up on Instagram about us when all the drama was going on that said: 'It's true, we don't have it as easy as ordinary couples. But baby, this is no ordinary kind of love.' I think that's spot on. I still think that's one of the sweetest things she wrote about us during our time together.

Being in the public eye definitely makes you more aware of how you're perceived and it's really frustrating when untrue things are said and people get a bad impression of you. I've never been that person who is desperate to be liked by everyone and not everyone in this world is going to be best mates with each other, but I do hate it when I'm misrepresented.

I think being written and talked about makes me think a lot more about what I say and do at times, and it also makes me more aware of how I look because that's also under scrutiny.

Before, no-one apart from me cared if I gained or lost weight, or whether I had a six-pack or not, but when you're in the public eye it's kind of expected that you keep yourself in decent shape. Especially if you're doing things like photo shoots and calendars.

As well as collaborating on our single, Kem and I also released a fitness DVD together and it was called *100% Fit* and it was honestly one of the funniest things I've ever done. We filmed it at the end of September once we'd wrapped on *Straight Outta Love Island.*

We filmed it over two days and it was tiring but Shona, the fitness guru we worked with, was unreal.

Kem and I weren't as fit as we usually are when we filmed it so hopefully that means people can relate to it. It wasn't like we found it really easy. We had to work at it too and you can see that on the DVD.

I was definitely in better shape before I went into *Love Island* than I am now, mainly because I worked out loads in the run-up because I was so aware I was going to spend a lot of time in swimming shorts. I do enjoy working out and when you see good results it motivates you, and I'd been getting in really good shape so I wanted to keep that up.

I did work out a little bit while I was in *Love Island*, but definitely not enough, and I haven't been to the gym once since I left, so my body does look different to how it did last summer and I'm conscious of that. I'm a bit weird because if I stop going to the gym I lose weight instead of gaining it. It can be hard for me to put weight on and I have been self-conscious about being too skinny in the past. It's said that you lose muscle eight times faster than you gain it. I reckon that's true because people kept coming up to me after the show saying 'You're much skinnier than I thought you would be.'

If I had the time I would definitely go to the gym more.

Once I find my motivation I can build back up again pretty quickly. I agree that a healthy body equals a healthy mind. Being in good nick does make me feel good about myself.

When I shot my 2018 calendar I wasn't that happy with the shape I was in. The shoot happened two or three weeks after *Love Island* so people may look at it and think I was in good shape. But I'm very critical of how I look and I knew that just a month before that I looked better. It's very easy to put ourselves down and I've never had a problem with low self-esteem, but I do feel better when I'm toned.

I've done photo shoots recently where magazines have asked me if I want to take my top off, and I really don't at the moment. I certainly wouldn't volunteer to do a topless picture. I feel like I'm all skin and bones. When that's pointed out to you by people you can start to feel a little bit paranoid.

I didn't have massive body issues when I was growing up but I wasn't the type to parade around a beach feeling like a god. Right now I definitely wouldn't feel great about sitting around a pool with people looking at me. I don't know if it's wrong to admit that but that's honestly how I feel.

I have had several times where I've worried about my weight though. First in my mid-teens I really wanted to be skinny because I hoped to become a jump jockey. Then when I realised that wasn't going to happen I started playing more football and put on a lot of muscle. I got in good shape but when I work out and bulk up, the muscles in my neck expand and it gets thicker, and that happened this time. It changed my entire face and I didn't like how I looked. At that point I thought I looked too big.

Although I enjoy working out I have to be really careful because my traps get really big and it all goes a bit Arnold

Schwarzenegger. When I'm slimmer and I'm not working out my face and my neck photograph so much better. But if I'm taking my top off for a shoot I want to have a six-pack. I need to find that happy medium between working out and still keeping my neck looking vaguely normal.

In an ideal world I'd like to do two good gym sessions a week. When I'm really busy and I don't have the time, it's not just exercise that I find hard to fit in, even my food goes off the rails a bit too. If I'm travelling around a lot I have to grab what I can where I can. If I'm on a photo shoot or a TV show I have to eat whatever is in catering.

I've always had a decent appetite and when I was working out a lot I tried to eat all the right foods to build muscles and still stay lean. But there are times now when I'll grab a bar of chocolate if I'm tired, rather than eating something that's good for me. I could definitely eat better generally and I'm working on it. If you're eating well you look much healthier, even if you're not exercising much.

There has always been masses of pressure on women to look perfect, but I do think it's getting bad for men too because of social media. I know some guys who follow Instagram accounts of personal trainers or fitness models and then they feel shit when they see all their chiselled jaws and perfect bodies. I do get it, I just try not to follow too many of those people!

Men's grooming is a much bigger deal now and stuff like tanning and skincare is more geared towards guys. I think it's a good thing and it encourages guys to take good care of themselves. My dad would never go near any of that stuff. He gets his hair cut once in a blue moon, would never use a moisturiser and he would not have a clue what to do with fake tan. But it's the norm for my generation.

Blokes are much more into looking after themselves now and with that comes more expectation. I pluck my own eyebrows (not as badly as I did as a teenager) and I shave and I used to fake-tan a bit, but I'm less bothered about all that stuff than I used to be. I'm surprised at myself because now I'm in the public eye and being looked at I should be upping my game and getting everything done beauty-wise, but I'm not that fussed. I reckon I kept my eyebrows in better shape before I was famous.

I know I'm very lucky because if I was a woman how I look would be talked about much more. Especially the fact I've lost weight. If I was female I'd be on the front covers of magazines and people would be asking what's wrong with me or if I'm eating enough. It would be the same if I suddenly put on weight.

Women are made to feel like they've done something wrong if they're a bit out of shape, so in that way I feel really grateful that there isn't as much speculation over what's going on underneath my clothes.

I feel bad for young girls especially because there's more pressure than ever on them to look 'perfect'. They look at girls in magazines and they don't think about the fact that they've had their hair and make-up done, an amazing photographer has taken their photo with brilliant lighting and then the shots have been airbrushed. They're just scanning the photos thinking 'Why am I not a size six and why isn't my skin flawless?'

It drives me mad when girls who are bigger than a size eight are called 'plus size' models. They're just models! Calling them plus size makes them sound like they're overweight, but they're just normal women. Why don't slim models have a weight-specific title? They're all doing the same job.

None of us are perfect and the shape of your body and your size is down to so many different factors. Your metabolism plays a big part, as does genetics. You can work out a lot and be the best you can be, but at some point you have to accept that perfection doesn't exist. It makes me feel sad that more people aren't content with how they are and they don't feel happy in their own skin. I'm not the best I can be at the moment and I know I can look better, but I try not to give myself *too* much of a hard time.

My body does fluctuate but I have to go with it. I don't always *love* it but that's part and parcel of being human. I'm so comfortable in my own skin as a rule that I'm happy with whatever. I've always been like that. I've never gone out of my way to impress people and it's not important for me to have loads of designer clothes and flash watches or cars.

I think I get that from my dad. He's worked hard for what he's got but he doesn't show it off. He could drive nice cars and wear expensive watches if he wanted to but he's never needed it. He would hate for someone to look at him and think he was flaunting what he's got.

He's so good with money: if a company was charging him a few quid more each month for a bill he'd phone up and haggle with them. He doesn't take having money for granted. He's a really good role model.

I know people who like others knowing they're on a good wage and it's rubbish because they rely on money to feel good. I know one guy who is constantly looking at the time so everyone notices he's got a Rolex. But actually all people notice is that he wants people to notice his Rolex, so he looks like a bit of a dick. I think that having to do things like that is a massive sign of insecurity, and I've never had issues in that area.

I'm now in an industry where showing off is second nature to a lot of the people in it, and everyone's trying to compete. The thing is, it's not like you get famous and you're instantly wealthy. Some people in the public eye are buying things they can't really afford just to look good in photos. Or they're wearing fakes.

I've been on the red carpet in £10 T-shirts but who cares? So much of the entertainment world is about portraying a certain kind of lifestyle but a lot of it is about smoke and mirrors. Some people are pretending to be something they're not, whereas I'll be happy to turn up at an event in trainers if I fancy it.

Honestly, you should have seen some of the cars I drove around in before *Love Island*. You'd have wondered how they were still running. They had bits hanging off them and scratches and dents from previous owners. But it didn't bother me that people would assume I was broke because I was driving such a shitheap.

I bought a battered old car for £250 about a year ago and when I went to pick my mate Josh up he was like 'What the hell is that?' He thought it was hilarious, and so did I. That car was no reflection on who I am as a person. And it ran bloody well so I was well chuffed to get such a bargain. That's me all over.

I do think the younger generation are much more image-conscious and self-conscious than I was at their age. Sometimes people will take photos with me and when they post them online they'll cover their faces with an emoji because they don't look perfect in the picture.

I do take a lot of selfies but they don't all have to be perfect and I don't care how many people like them. I don't mind if I look a bit dodgy in some of them. I really like candid photos, and even if someone takes a picture of me at a bad angle or something, I would never ask them to take it down. I am what I am. I put up a ropey picture once and I got loads of people telling me I looked awful, which we can all do without, but fuck it.

· · · · ·

There's a lot more pressure on kids in general. I was quite late with certain things, especially girls, but these days kids are having sex younger and younger and it's becoming normal. Kids have phones at ten and they can access porn really easily. I know kids are getting phones younger for safety now and I do understand that, but they've become like an extension of them. And you can access anything online and that's scary. It's hard for kids to be innocent.

I didn't have a phone until I was seventeen, which is mad, but I was happy about that. I liked my own company and I didn't want to be on the phone all the time. I saw my mates enough at school and college. Even now I'm terrible at replying to messages. At the moment I've got thirty-five unread text messages, forty-two unread WhatsApp messages and 217 unread Facebook messages – and they are just the ones from people I actually know. On top of that I've got Facebook, Twitter and Instagram. I would never get anything done if I replied to everything, and I totally get why kids are glued to their phones. If someone needs to get hold of me that badly, they can call me.

The best thing about phones is that people can get hold of

you at any time, and the worst thing about phones is that people can get hold of you at any time.

I have a love/hate relationship with mine, and Katie Price certainly hasn't helped!

Some stuff that confuses me

People who take themselves too seriously. Some people can be so cautious and think about everything they say and I like people who just say what they feel. I find it weird when people think about every word that comes out of their mouths. I don't, clearly, and I know it sometimes gets me into trouble but I'm just being myself.

The River Nile. I got an A in geography at school but I still used to think the River Nile was in Nottingham. I thought that for years. But it's in Egypt, isn't it?

The world. I think this world is such a crazy place and the fact I've become who I am from a tiny egg is mental. The whole world is weird. How can you make sense of something as big as this?

Grown-up cartoons. Why do people watch them and laugh out loud? They're not that funny. I don't get it. Cartoons are for kids.

Timekeeping. I don't understand why I can never be on time. Being late is my worst habit.

Reincarnation. I know that's a bit heavy but I do think when you pass away you come back as someone else. I think I've already lived before and I'm adamant I was an elephant. I don't know why, I just feel like I was. Olivia says she thinks I was probably a sloth because I'm a human sloth now.

I think I'll be a polar bear in my next life. Imagine me on a slab of ice hanging out with some walruses. I'm a very good swimmer and I reckon I'd be a good hunter, so I'd make a perfect polar bear.

The beginning of the world. I would love to know how everything started. How do things grow? How are there so many species of animals? How did they become what they are? What did they start off as? I could go on asking questions for ever. I wish someone would hand me a manual that explains it all really simply.

Our bodies. How do our bodies work? Seriously? There's so much going on inside us and it's so complicated. I wonder why everything wasn't made really straightforward. There are millions of different illnesses you can get. Who thought all of those up? It must have taken so much time.

10

Keep Calm and Carry On

Needless to say, there have been moments here and there when being famous has felt a bit overwhelming for me. Thankfully now I know how to deal with it better, but there have been times when I've had to take myself out of the entertainment world and reassess things.

There is a certain amount of pressure that comes with being in the public eye and sometimes that manifests itself as anxiety. I was lying on my bed quite recently and all of a sudden my breathing started becoming more rapid for absolutely no reason and it was scary. I have those days when my head gets busy and I question things that wouldn't normally bother me.

I also broke down while I was playing cricket not that long ago. I was out on the field and I burst into tears. It was proper weird. People must have looked at me and thought 'What the hell is he doing?'

I got upset because for a brief moment I felt like I couldn't get a grip on it. I had to go off the field and sit down for twenty minutes because I was properly shaken up. I did go back on and play eventually but I had to take that time out. I think that's one of the hardest things for me; how unpredictable anxiety can be.

I know that I'm stronger mentally than I've ever been and I've found ways to deal with the difficult times, including using the techniques that David Crees taught me back in the day. I'm not totally anxiety-free but I can handle it better when it comes on because I've learned how to. One of the best things I can do is speak to Olivia about it and tell her I'm feeling shit. She'll sit with me for as long as it takes for me to feel better.

There's no point in keeping it to myself. Those kinds of things always catch up with you. You can't keep running from your problems because they'll keep chasing, and eventually they'll overtake you. If you don't deal with your feelings they can fester and come out as anger or full-on depression.

Once you start to talk about it you realise that there are a lot more people suffering with it. I had no idea that some of my mates were feeling the same way I was, but thankfully it's becoming less of a stigma.

What I've realised as I've got a bit older is that actually not feeling normal is normal in this day and age. Everyone goes through stuff, whatever job you do or walk of life you come from.

• • • • •

On 10 October 2016, which was World Mental Health Day, I put out a tweet thanking David for helping me. When I was in *Love Island* the press picked up on that post and reprinted it. They also picked up on the fact that I was quite emotional while I was in *Love Island*, and very open about my feelings.

As a result of the press coverage, CALM – Campaign Against Living Miserably – got in touch and asked me if I would be interested in working with them as an ambassador. It was such a great moment.

CALM run a mental health helpline that has helped so many people who are suffering, and I was so lucky they asked me to come on board to help raise awareness. The person on the other end of the phone may be a stranger but they understand and empathise with what you're going through. If I'd known there was a service like that when I was going through a really bad time I would definitely have used it. That's why it was a big deal for me to let other people know who the charity are and that they want to help. They understand and they don't judge.

CALM are trying to get rid of the idea that men should bottle up their emotions and get on with things. It's the worst thing you can do. I know from personal experience that what helped me was the exact opposite. The more I tried to keep it all in, the worse things got.

There's this perception that men should be the strong ones in a family. They should take charge, provide for their family and never show their flaws. It's a stereotype that needs to be challenged.

Here come the statistics: some 84 per cent of men bottle up their emotions and don't tell anyone when they're having mental health issues, which is a massive, scary number. That's over four in every five people.

There are twelve male suicides in the UK every single day. Not attempted suicides, actual suicides. That's almost a whole Super League team every twenty-four hours.

Three in four suicides in the UK are male and it's the biggest killer in men under the age of forty-five. It's not cancer and it's not heart attacks, it's suicides. Those stats are horrifying. Imagine how desperate all those poor guys feel. I know it's horrible to hear about it but being honest and having a wider conversation about it is the only way things are going to change.

We're all different. Some of us are more sensitive than others, and no one should ever have to put on a front because they're worried about what other people will think of them.

I get such nice messages from people on Twitter saying that what I'm doing has really helped them to overcome things through the campaign.

One guy PMd me and said: 'Success and exposure through reality TV are often looked down upon and needlessly judged, but it's such an amazing thing you're doing. By using your success in such a selfless way and helping people in my situation without actually knowing you're doing it. So I'm really grateful for that. You give people like me hope and I hope you're aware of that.' Messages like that are incredible.

• • • • •

What CALM want people to understand is that when they're suffering, a lot of people are going through the same kind of things. People do come out the other side and get better and have a healthier state of mind. An illness needs treating, and just because people can't see what's wrong with you on the outside it doesn't mean it isn't all going on inside.

CALM did an amazing campaign to tie in with International Men's Day last May called Change The Picture. The aim was to get people talking about men, masculinity and mental health, and they invited both amateur and professional photographers to send in photos that challenged male stereo-types.

They held an exhibition at the Getty Images Gallery in London and it was honestly amazing. The images were so powerful. One of them was a selfie of this guy who looked like any other guy you'd see walking down the street, but he was suffering from extreme loneliness. And even though it wasn't obvious when you looked at him, it was all going on inside.

I'm probably not a typical example of what a man is supposed to be. I'm shit at mending things, I don't mind cooking (even though I'm not very good at it) and I cry if I feel like it. And that's not something I will ever be ashamed of. I am what I am.

· · · · ·

I did a Topman campaign with CALM and it was honestly one of the best things I've ever done in my life. When I was asked to become an ambassador for Topman that was mind-blowing enough. I was the first reality star ever to be a brand ambassador for Topman. In the past they've used sports stars, musicians and actors, so it was crazy. But the campaign was next level.

When they told me about the concept I loved it straight away. The plan was for us to launch the campaign over two days. On the first day, 10 November, we were set to release an advertisement for L'Eau de Chris, the first ever bottled water infused with real tears. My tears. And on the second day, we'd do the big reveal and explain what it was really all about.

I uploaded a topless black and white shot of me holding the bottle of water on to Instagram and I got so much stick. I got death threats and everything. Someone told me I needed to be shot for being arrogant enough to think anyone would want to buy water with my tears in it. Someone wrote 'What has this world become when some reality star thinks they're that important'. People thought it was a serious product launch and I was mocked mercilessly. But that's exactly what we were hoping for. We wanted to create a big talking point, and we definitely did.

It was uncomfortable at times and the comments actually made me feel quite anxious because it was pure abuse. But I knew I just had to hold my nerve until the truth came out. I stopped reading the comments completely because some of them were so vitriolic. I had no idea people could get so worked up over water.

The following day Topman invited fifty members of the press to come down to their flagship Oxford Street store for the official unveiling of the water. They set up a little stage and streamed the event via Facebook Live at 8.15 a.m. That's when they broke the news that the real name of the campaign was 'Ludicrous', because it's ludicrous that people bottle up their emotions. The reaction on people's faces was priceless.

There were fifty bottles of water made in total and each one was genuinely infused with real tears. We captured my tears in a little bottle and that went off to a factory to be bottled. Those were given out to each member of the press who came to the launch and I also got to take one home. It's got pride of place in my flat.

Topman's involvement included them donating £2 from every pair of boxer shorts that were sold that month to the charity to help them to reach more people and keep the help-lines going, and they raised loads of money.

I spent all day doing press in support of the campaign. I was live on *Sky News* and I did loads of radio interviews. I also did a speech to about 150 people at the HAVAS building in London, which was nerve-wracking but allowed me to answer any questions people had. Some of the campaign images were projected onto buildings in London that night, and my photo was featured on roundabouts and taxis around the capital. If you'd told me one day I would be involved in something that big I wouldn't have believed it.

It was incredible how quickly things turned around. I got so many supportive tweets it was hard to keep up. I got a crazy number of nice comments from people saying they'd misjudged me. I also had PMs from people who admitted they'd tried to commit suicide in the past and they were still overcoming their problems, but that they felt better because it was more out in the open now.

Some girls messaged me saying that their boyfriends had been suffering from mental health issues and the campaign provided a way to talk to them about it.

I had so much interaction on social media and I was so happy because it showed that we'd got the message across, which was our aim. Ultimately we wanted to get people discussing the campaign as much as possible. Without wanting to sound like a twat, I wanted to use my platform to encourage others to speak out. I really hope it's helped a lot of people.

I admire people who are upfront about their issues. There's a reason self-help, anxiety and addiction books are bestsellers around the world, and they're a brilliant place to start if you're not ready to talk to someone just yet. And when you are ready, CALM are there.

I've been really lucky that I've done good campaigns and worked with great companies and people want to associate with me, and it's nice to have those opportunities. I really want that to continue and, as cheesy as it may sound, I'd really like to carry on helping people wherever I can.

· · · · ·

After the Katie Price debacle, the *Sun* newspaper were really gunning for me. I felt like they were out to get me in any way they could and I woke up one morning to find that they'd printed a story making out I'd been racist.

Olivia had filmed me rapping along to a Drake song in a club and then posted it on her Instagram stories. The lyrics featured the N-word, and because I had repeated those lyrics they turned it into a big story. I was so upset. I understand why some people were annoyed but I would never ever say or do something that I would consider to be offensive so it really got to me.

I issued an apology on Twitter. Some people were giving me shit for it and other people were saying it was ridiculous that I'd had to apologise. I felt like I was being stitched up as payback for standing up for myself. I couldn't stop thinking about it all weekend and I couldn't bring myself to check Twitter in case everyone was laying into me. Mario from *TOWIE* stuck up for me and he got bare abuse for it because people are so in your business they start having a go at the people around you too.

Mario is a really good guy. He's best mates with one of my managers, Chris, because they went to school together, and we got on brilliantly from day one. He's also been really helpful and given me some good advice. He's been in the industry for a long time and he's had his ups and downs, so he gets it.

Ollie Proudlock is someone else who's become a really close friend. We met at a Vodafone event and we chatted for ages and we've been mates ever since. We speak most days now and we did a social campaign for McDonalds together. His girl-friend is one of the nicest people ever.

Aside from my mates from back when, Mario, Jamie, Joey Essex and Jamie Laing are the guys I see the most of now. I'm careful about getting close to too many people and trying to be friends with everyone and be part of a big gang – I'm selective – but I like who I like.

The only opinions that count are my friends' and my family's. I know I can trust the people close to me and that means everything. If one of them stitched me up I would be devas-tated. To be betrayed like that would be the end for me. I think I would lose faith in humanity.

· · · · ·

I'm more switched on these days and I've learnt my lessons and I don't listen to everything the gossip columns say about me. It's not ideal because we just want to be ourselves; we just have to be more careful now.

I also keep my cool more than I used to. Sometimes when I'm stood in front of a bank of paps they'll start shouting things out to get a reaction so they get a more interesting shot of me. They're desperate to get pictures of me looking really pissed off because they can probably sell them for more money.

I've had paps taking the piss out of me, asking me what I think of Katie Price, or insulting Olivia. All sorts. I used to want to tell them to fuck off but now I stand and smile for as long as I need to, and then I walk away and forget about it. It is what it is.

I've had several big nights out since becoming famous and there have been times when I've gone out and had a few too many and some shit pap photos have been taken. It's usually when the drinks are free and it's hard to keep track of how much you've had. All of a sudden it creeps up on me and I realise I've had way too much.

I'm a bit of a nightmare if I drink too much. I go past the point of knowing what I'm doing and it always ends up badly and I'll wake up full of regret about what I've done the night before.

One of those times was in December when I went on a night out and a guy I got talking to was filming me on his mobile outside a club. I was hammered and he was asking me about mine and Kem's single and I was bantering and I made a few stupid comments about some other musical artists. I was so drunk I don't even remember, and didn't even realise he was filming me.

Apparently I was talking to the guy filming me for about half an hour and he even lent me his coat because I was cold while I was waiting for a cab. My friends I was with thought he was my mate so they didn't think anything of it. Then he went and sold the video to a newspaper.

Loads of guys go out on a weekend and get drunk and say stupid things, but obviously someone can make money from me doing that. It was well cringe when I saw the video. I was also really sad that someone would use me in that way and stitch me up for a bit of money.

It's horrible that I have to be so careful about who I trust but I have been stung, and it's made me feel shit. I would rather miss out on good nights out than risk being put in that position again.

The worst thing is when you've got a cracking hangover and your manager calls you to tell you the press have got a story on you and they're going to run it. It makes me feel sick and my anxiety goes through the roof until I can calm myself down again. It's the most awful feeling ever.

I do try to moderate myself a lot more now and if I have been drinking I'm much more careful about what I do. I liked a girl's photo on Twitter at 1 a.m. after a night out in January when I was looking through Instagram and I didn't mean anything by it. The next day there was a story in the papers about how I'd liked another girl's 'photos'. It was one picture and I unliked it five minutes later. It's ridiculous that people are so on the case looking for negative stories on me that the fact I liked one photo for five minutes turned into a big deal. It drives me a bit mad having to watch everything I do, but that's the way it is now.

It's not like it only happens to me. We've all seen things that celebs have tweeted and then taken down within seconds. But those seconds are long enough for someone to do a screen grab and get it into the press. It's incredible. There is no hiding if you make a mistake on social media.

Thankfully my managers are really understanding. I'm actually thinking of going to see a counsellor about it so I can find new ways to deal with it. I'm still equipped with all the tools I learned from David Crees, but this is a totally new area for me. It doesn't happen that often but when things are really bad I can't eat for days.

I don't want to be less trusting of people and have to watch my back at all times, but that's the way it is. Nights out for me from now on will be about going out with mates I know I can totally trust to places where I won't get papped if I come out drunk, like my local pub back home.

I've had to learn my lessons pretty quickly but I think it would be good to go and speak to a professional about how to handle life in the spotlight. Some people find it really easy but I think because I'm sensitive things do get to me more than they would other people.

* * * * *

I'm definitely not at celebrity parties every night. I go to things that are important for work but other than that I'm usually at home in my onesie watching TV. I work such long days that often by the time I get back at night I'm too tired to go out again. I really enjoy having my downtime with Olivia, and I get much more enjoyment out of being at home chilling than I do going on a big one.

I can completely see how people can let being 'famous' run away with them but I genuinely think I'm too grounded to do that. It would be easy to get up a head of steam and start thinking you're something you're not. But I know who I am. I'm just a kid from the Cotswolds who loves cows and shit. I'll always be that kid.

You could never change me as a person. I'm not going to dump my old mates and start going clubbing every night and trying to be mates with celebs. I try to be friendly and approachable like I've always been. It's not like I went on *Love Island* and had a complete personality transplant.

My family would be the first ones to tell me if I ever started getting a big head. They'd never watched reality TV before

Love Island, and although they enjoyed it they don't think I'm some kind of superstar now. My brothers still take the piss out of me and we'll go down the pub and have a pint like we have done for many years.

Mum isn't rolling out a red carpet when I get home. She still expects me to clear up after myself and Dad sometimes asks me to help out on the farm. They're so normal. They never ask me about what I've been doing or who I've met because it's not on their radar. They want the best for me and they're happy if I'm happy. I'm still their son who gets a bit arsey when I'm hungry, and that's who I'll be for ever.

My friends also help to keep me really grounded. I still hang out with the same people and they're all really happy for me. No one has acted jealously or been bitter that I'm doing what I am. Not one of my mates has given me any shit for anything. They might take the piss out of me for being famous every now and again, and they find it ridiculous if we're out and someone asks for a selfie, but they're massively supportive.

I have made a few new friends in the industry now but I'm a good judge of character and I would never become mates with someone just because of who they are or because they're famous. That's not me at all. It's about picking out the good people.

It is very surreal that I'm now friends with some of the sportsmen I idolised growing up because I didn't ever imagine that happening. But they're all such nice people and it is really good to have people to talk to who properly get it.

· · · · ·

If you believe the press, Olivia and I were splitting up every five minutes, but people can read too much into a tweet or a photo and assume you've broken up because of a little comment. We seemed to be 'on the rocks' every day, according to certain websites. We'd had a few breaks here and there but it was never anything serious.

There was a big drama over some photos of Olivia on a night out at a club with her ex back when we first left *Love Island*, and the press really went to town with those. Liv and this guy were chatting and some people thought they looked too close, and all of a sudden everyone was saying she was back with him and we'd broken up.

I saw Olivia immediately afterwards and everything was totally fine. It was a non-story. In the end I put a picture of us together up on Instagram as a bit of a 'fuck off' to the doubters.

I'm very aware that certain members of the press are desperate for Liv and me to break up. They're just waiting for that moment when they can write a big headline saying we've called it a day. And ultimately, eventually they got it. Do I think the pressure of the press anf the public was a factor in our split? Without a doubt.

So many people doubted Olivia and I but in my eyes we were the most real couple out there. We used to get a lot of people giving us shit on social media and saying we were fake but that did change over time. It got to the point where I got more likes on photos of Olivia and me together than I did of ones of me on my own, which was really sweet.

Despite that, because social media is a double-edged sword, I also had messages from people telling me that I should dump Olivia right up until we split. Sometimes I have to block out the noise from other people and the only way to do that is to distance myself from the likes of Twitter and Instagram when I need to. Nowadays when I post I don't read all of the comments like I used to. I've got 1.9 million followers so there are always going to be people who are negative, and sometimes you just don't need it.

Relationships are hard enough and stuff like that doesn't make it easier.

It is definitely trickier holding down a relationship when you're both well known, and Olivia and I both knew that maybe it wasn't going to be an easy ride. But we really did think we could make it. I guess we'll never have a chance to find out if things would have been different if we weren't in the public eye. Maybe if there was less focus on our relationship it would have made it simpler and we'd still be togther now. Who knows?

Both Liv and I were really sad when Amber and Kem split up but we both knew it was on the cards for a little while before the story came out in the papers. I'd known for about three weeks beforehand that it was potentially happening and it was a real shame because Olivia and I are really close to them. Not everything is meant to be and they've both got a lot to focus on with their careers at the moment.

Amber and Olivia are still good mates and Kem and I are still well close and it's fine. Amber and I are never going to be best friends. I hardly ever see her but when I do we say hello. There's no drama.

I don't think their break-up put more pressure on Olivia and me because it's always been there anyway. It's constant so it's not like everyone suddenly thought 'I wonder if they'll be next?' The media had been hinting about it for months anyway so it didn't add anything.

A lot of rumours started circling about us breaking up again when I was caught on camera hugging a girl in a club. But that's literally all I was doing. I was chatting to the girl and we looked close because I was leaning in to talk to her because the music was so loud. The guy who videoed me uploaded it to his Twitter account and when I looked at his profile he was a journalist, so I wonder if it was a set-up. Nothing happened between us but obviously it looked really bad.

Liv phoned me the day the story came out and asked if I'd seen it. Then she said, 'Have you got anything to say about it?' and she put the phone down.

I do get it. I shouldn't have had my arms around a girl, but I'd drunk too much and I got closer than I should have done. But that's as far as it went.

It was reported that Liv and I properly split up over it but we didn't. She did take time away from our relationship to think, but then she admitted that it was twisted to sound like she'd dumped me. She had a bit of time to herself to think and we talked everything through and it was totally fine within a couple of days. It wasn't as dramatic as it was made out to be.

I am much more conscious of what I do when I'm out when there are girls around now. I had a night out with some mates and my management in London a while back, and this girl came over to our booth and asked to have her photo taken with me. I had a quick snap and then we started chatting, and even though it was totally innocent I did think 'I can see the headlines – "Chris talks to tall blonde girl in nightclub behind Liv's back"'. We were only having a conversation but I was really wary.

She asked if she could take a video of us together because she was applying for *Love Island* and wanted me to record a message saying that the producers should put her in. I felt well bad but I said no because I didn't feel comfortable about it. I knew that if she put it on social media it could have been taken the wrong way.

I try my hardest to be nice and polite when people come up to me but you can't please everyone all of the time. You don't always know what someone's motivations are, so the bottom line is that sometimes you have to think the worst to protect yourself.

That's another thing fame has taught me. No matter how hard you try to be a good person, in life you will always piss some people off. That's the way it goes.

It's strange to think that a year ago I could have been sat in a pub with all my mates and no one would have given a shit about me. I could have stripped off and danced on the bar and the only comeback would be a lot of mickey-taking from my mates. But now? Aside from getting absolutely bollocked by my management team, that kind of thing could also affect everything about my career, which I am well keen to keep working on.

My world has changed and it took a while for my head to realise just how much, hence I've made a few mistakes here and there. But you live and learn.

• • • • •

Olivia and I didn't ever hide the fact that our relationship wasn't all hearts and flowers. There were days when things weren't great because we'd had a stupid argument, and because we're both stubborn, arguments dragged on a bit. Neither of us wanted to apologise first but we would work it out eventually.

Our stubbornness drove each other mad at times and we

did wind each other up, but at some point one person has to go and cuddle the other one and make it all right, don't they? The rows, which could be about anything from the mess in the flat to where we were going to go out to eat, didn't ever last long. We knew that we argued over ridiculous things, but don't all couples?

We were like best mates as well as girlfriend and boyfriend.

Olivia used to say that we were obsessed with each other and I agree.

· · · · ·

When Olivia and I found out we were being given our own reality show we were over the moon. We started filming in December 2017 and it was brilliant to begin with. I'd just moved into a new place and because we were filming together it meant that we got to spend loads of time in each other's company, which we both loved.

Olivia and I found out about the show when we were invited for a meeting at ITV. We didn't know what it was about but we were excited because we thought it must be something pretty big.

We met with a couple of producers and they said they really liked the way we came across on screen on *Straight Outta Love Island*. They explained that they wanted it to be a fly-on-the-wall reality show called *Crackin' On* based around our day-to-day lives, and we absolutely loved the idea.

Liv and I went out for a meal that night to celebrate, and we had to keep the whole thing top secret for two months, which was hard. It was like going through the *Love Island* process all over again. I was desperate to tell people but we had to be really discreet.

We weren't worried about doing the show, or about it affecting our relationship, at all. We didn't act any differently when we were on camera to when we weren't. What people saw is real. There were times when we argued a lot, but that's why people are invested in us, because we were always honest.

We moved house the same week we started filming the show so that was quite stressful because we were trying to sort out new furniture and get organised. (Anyone who's seen the show will know how well that went. I think it's fair to say that Liv and I have quite different tastes.) But it was also a relief to leave the old place behind and go somewhere where we knew the paps wouldn't be able to take pictures of us whenever they fancied it.

The move was quite stressful because we literally moved into the new place with nothing. Olivia owns the old place we were living in, as well as all the furniture, and she left it all there so we were starting from zero.

I bought loads of things I've never imagined myself buying, like bins and washing powder. I did a massive Amazon order and when all the stuff arrived I felt well domesticated. I can even work the dishwasher on my own. I feel a bit like 'I've got this.'

I ordered a washing machine but, because I was going to be away when it was arriving, I got it delivered to my parents' house in the Cotswolds. I didn't realise how big they are and when I went to pick it up it wouldn't fit in the car. It was well annoying. I had to get someone to drop it off in a van in the end.

When we first moved in Olivia divided her time between both places but she stayed back at hers a lot if she wanted to get a decent night's sleep or if we fell out, so I was often on my own.

It did kind of annoy me at first that Olivia and I weren't properly living together in the new place, but after a while I was like 'Fuck it. If that's what we need to do to get our relationship back on track, so be it.' That became more of a regular occurence as time went on, which says a lot. I think Olivia only stayed in the flat with me for five days in total by the time we broke up I felt like I was already lived on my own. It was like I had a bachelor pad even though I'm going out with someone, which was weird.

The show was both fun and full-on to film in the beginning, but it got easier as time went on and we settled into everything. Obviously we had a lot of cameras around us but we're both so used to that now it didn't bother us, and we got to be in each other's company more than we had for a while, so that was brilliant.

The show is proper reality so of course, standard, we did fall out quite a lot. We both found it hard to tone it down for the cameras because we can't be anything but ourselves. If we discussed something one of us didn't want to talk about there was a lot of tension. It was a bit like being in the villa and we forgot there were cameras around, so we didn't hold back.

We even fell out when we went on a break to Amsterdam. We argued in the taxi on the way to the airport about an Instagram video I saw of Olivia where she was drunk in a club and chatting to two guys. I was narked about it and her excuse was 'I was pissed.' If that had been the other way around I would have got slaughtered for doing the same thing, but in the end I had to let it go so we could enjoy the trip.

Aside from that one argument, Amsterdam was really good fun. We had a right laugh and we headed to the red-light district and went to a peep show. Olivia was horrified by it though. I'd thought she would think it was good banter but she wasn't keen, which is fair enough.

Filming was both stressful and fun, but we'd agreed to let the cameras into our lives so we couldn't then decide what we did and didn't want them to film. We did lose our privacy but we were under no illusion that that was what was going to happen. You don't sign up to do a reality show and then expect people to keep their noses out of your business. If you argue on camera it becomes everyone else's business.

It's when things happen in private and then end up in the press that I find it hard, but I guess you can't really have it both ways. You're either in or you're out.

A lot was made about the fact that Olivia and I didn't spend that much time together over Christmas and New Year but, honestly, there was nothing to it and I think we both just needed some time out to relax and get our heads together. I went off to the Cotswolds and had a much-needed two weeks off, and Liv got to hang out with her friends and family.

Because we didn't post any photos of us together on social media the press were phoning our management companies to see if we'd split up, and some fans even phoned my manager to ask if we were still together. But there wasn't there wasn't anything to it and we were still a couple. It was just good for us to feel 'normal' for a bit again. It may have seemed like it was quite a shit period for us but we kept in touch a lot so it wasn't like we ignored each other for that time.

We also spent a lot of time together in the lead-up to Christmas. Olivia organised a big surprise party for my twenty-fifth on 22 December at a bar in London. She made a massive effort and I was so touched. She even started a WhatsApp group so everyone knew what was going on.

Loads of my old mates from back home came, as well as my brothers and my parents. There were quite a few different circles of mates, including new friends I've made like Joey Essex and Mario Falcone, and it was nice to get them all together.

I wasn't actually feeling very well on the day but I went and played golf with my dad in the morning and felt a bit better, and then as soon as I arrived at the venue and saw everyone I perked right up. Liv got me this amazing cake with a marzipan figurine on top of me with a sheep, but she was horrified when her mate Georgia pulled my head off. Then one of my mates thought it would be funny to eat my head and she was well upset. I think it's fair to say everyone had a fair few drinks that night.

I went back to the Cotswolds the day after the party and I was so content chilling out when I got back home – I didn't want to do anything. I was going to bed at 1 a.m. or 2 a.m. and sleeping until 3 or 4 p.m. some days. My mum probably felt like I was going through my teenage years again.

That's when I realised that the more sleep you have the more tired you become. Or maybe I just slept way, way too much. I was in bed pretty much all the time but I was still tired the whole time. I'd probably built up a bit of a sleep debt over the few months before, so it was a real leap going from four hours' sleep a night to fourteen.

I didn't have to worry about getting papped and I knew that if I went to the local supermarket there was no chance there was going to be a photographer lurking around. Sometimes I didn't see anyone apart from my family for days at a time and I think it's important to have balance in your life.

Christmas was pretty standard but really nice. We had the family round and ate a lot. No one treated me any differently from the way they always do. A few of my extended family asked me questions about what I'd been up to but no one quizzed me or anything. They're not bothered about it all.

I didn't get loads of presents from my parents that year. They probably think I'm earning enough to buy my own shit now! Liv got me a load of men's Clarins products and a Gucci wallet. She tried to get me a Louis Vuitton rucksack from Harrods but they'd sold out, and I don't reckon there's much chance of her getting me one now.

I thought long and hard about what to buy Liv and in the end I got her a nude-coloured Chanel handbag and a picture frame with a photo of me in it. Only kidding, that would be awful, it was actually a photo of both of us.

Olivia and I did do a lot of nice things for each other and I think the most romantic thing I did for her was when I bought her a Céline handbag just before I went to LA to film my show with Kem last year. I went to Harrods and chose it and I asked them to deliver it on a certain date.

I told Liv I had a really important delivery on that day, so she stayed in and waited for it. Obviously when it turned up it had her name on the box so when she opened it she saw this amazing bag. I even included a handwritten note and she was really touched.

The only time I went out back home was to go for food with my mates, but other than that I did a lot of chilling and watching TV. I went out for New Year but even that was quite laid-back.

I was going to go out with Joey Essex but I was feeling so lazy I couldn't be bothered to travel to London. It felt like a lot of effort. In the end I messaged a lad I'd known for years called Ben and he invited me to a party in Bristol. He and twenty-five of his mates rented out a big house that had loads of rooms and a swimming pool and shit. It was wicked.

I didn't know anyone apart from Ben but everyone was so friendly and I had a right laugh. Olivia phoned me at midnight so we kind of saw the New Year in together, but it wasn't like it was the end of the world that we didn't spend it together.

I got to bed at 8.30 a.m. and then I headed to Cheltenham races off the back of a couple of hours' sleep. I was absolutely knackered and I only managed to watch one race, but my mate Aidan Coleman won it, so happy days.

I slipped back into my old, normal, everyday life really quickly and I didn't miss being in the papers every day or getting papped. Like I've said before, attention isn't like air to me and I don't need it to survive. I don't get caught up in whether or not I'm in the gossip pages. I don't want fame badly enough that I don't mind people writing shit about me as long as they're writing about me. Do you get what I mean?

I was happy relaxing and chatting to the cows. They don't give a shit that I'm Chris from *Love Island*. It made me appreciate the farm so much more. I'd go to my brother Ben's log cabin and play Mario Kart on the Wii and I'd feel a million miles away from all the celebrity stuff.

Please don't think I'm moaning or being ungrateful. This is my job now and, as far as jobs go, mine is bloody great. And no job is perfect and there are always going to be things that annoy you about yours. Even if you're a supermodel you have to get on crazy flights and work when you're jetlagged. There are downsides to everything. I'm realistic about that. When you become famous life doesn't suddenly become perfect.

• • • • •

I knew my 'holiday' had to come to an end at some point and on 5 January I headed back to Surrey and Liv and I carried on filming *Crackin' On*. That's when Liv and I went to Amsterdam and posted the first photo of us together for ages. People started saying that we did it to prove that we were still together, but it really wasn't.

The thing with social media is that you're damned if you do and damned if you don't. If you live your relationship through it you get shit, and if you don't you get shit. Maybe we should be a bit more strategic and clever about it but we can't be bothered. Which leads me on to the next big thing that made the papers – our argument at the NTAs.

Did we have a fallout? Yes, that's no secret, but it wasn't as bad as was reported. Olivia wrote in her *New!* magazine column that we had a row because we didn't see a lot of each other, and that was true, but it only lasted for about three seconds and it certainly wasn't a big bust-up.

There was a story that we fell out because I was annoyed that she was flirting with some guy from *Hollyoaks* who I'd never even heard of. The story came out of absolutely nowhere and it made us both look muggy because she'd apparently been flirting behind my back, and I looked muggy because I'd got in a mood about it. But that did not happen and in the end the story got taken down from the newspaper's website.

Liv also claimed in her *New!* column that we argued because I'm not a good drunk, but I certainly wasn't hammered that night. I'd been presenting with Kem on the red carpet for ITV earlier in the evening so I didn't even drink that much. I wasn't excessively pissed and acting like a dick, which I will hold my hands up and say I have been guilty of in the past.

Liv and I had words about her mentioning my drinking. I thought it was a bit of a low blow so I lost my head. It ended up looking like the whole thing was my fault. We both drink too much sometimes but actually that night I kept things together.

A few of the papers made out I've got a drink problem. I'm already pretty paranoid about going out after what happened when that guy videoed me when I was battered, and now I'm even more mindful of how I behave so I don't end up in a similar situation. Now on top of that I also have to worry about people thinking I can't control my drinking, when actually I'm very happy to go out for a couple of beers and then call it a night. Like any lad I take things too far at times, but it's not like I'm on the lash every night being well rowdy. I hardly ever go out these days, but it feels like whenever I do something kicks off.

I knew I would see Katie Price at the NTAs too, but actually that turned out to be fine. Kem and I were on the red carpet and the cameras were switching from him and me to Roman Kemp, who was presenting next to us. Katie came over to us when we were off air. She didn't realise and she thought it was going out live, so she tried to talk to me to get some attention and I blanked her. She stroked my arm and told me to have a good night and she probably thought the press would pick up on it. She must have been gutted when she realised none of it aired.

It was so nice to work with Kem at the NTAs, especially as there were rumours going around that we'd had a turbulent friendship. When Kem and Amber were still together Amber told Olivia that Kem had said a couple of negative things about me, and of course it got back to me. But it was a bit like Chinese whispers and he didn't ever say anything to my face. Even if things were said, so what? I chose to ignore it and carry on. I was so unbothered by it.

From my point of view Kem and I have always had a good relationship. We've had a few niggles here and there and probably pissed each other off a bit at times like mates do, but we've never, ever argued. I went along and supported him in *Dancing on Ice* and he's been really supportive of what I'm doing.

I will never, ever forgive him for the time he called me Jake by mistake though. It's just not something I think I can ever get over. Basically, everyone was making a massive deal about the fact that Kem and Jake Quickenden had a bit of a bromance going on while they were doing *Dancing on Ice*. Then one day Kem and I and our managers were having coffee and Kem called me Jake. Yeah, I know.

He immediately put his hand over his mouth and looked absolutely horrified. His reaction was so extreme you would honestly have thought he'd called his girlfriend by another girl's name or something. I tweeted about it and everyone picked up on it. It was well funny.

There is honestly no jealousy there and it was all banter. I get on really well with Jake and he's such a nice guy. And you know, there's room for all three of us in our friendship.

I've learned so much about fame over the last year. I've learned that it isn't the be-all and end-all, but it's done me a lot of favours because it's taught me a lot. I've learned to hold my tongue more, I've learned that you can be put on a pedestal one day and pulled down by the press or social media the next, and I've learned that you can't take the industry too seriously.

Fame has definitely given me a tougher shell and made me more resilient. It used to really affect me when there was anything negative written about me in the media and I always questioned why someone would say something nasty, but now I don't read stuff. I used to google my name and see what was being written about me but that wasn't at all healthy, so I stopped. Now if I see stuff, I see it, but I don't go searching for it.

I still feel anxious if I find out a story about me is going to be in the papers because I don't know what's going to be said and if things are going to be twisted, but it's nowhere near as bad as it used to be. I try to be more grounded about it now and tell myself that in the grand scheme of things it's not a big deal. The world isn't going to end if someone writes something bad about me.

Looking back at my time in the industry so far there's nothing I would do differently. Even though I may not have handled every tricky situation in the best way it's all got me to where I am. And, if it's not too much of a cliché, made me who I am. Should I have shut my mouth when I was wound up? Probably. But what's done is done.

I would like to stay in this industry for as long as possible and have some longevity, so I think it's good that I've learned things the hard way early on. I'm going to carry on working hard and see where things take me and hopefully doors will open and the opportunities will come.

• • • • •

I do think about the future for Liv and me. Of course I do. I'm twenty-five and Olivia is twenty-six and we know what we want. We're both doing well and we want to be sensible with our money, build a solid future for ourselves and do all the things couples dream of doing. That's my biggest goal. It's bigger than anything else I'm doing right now. I'm not saying it has to happen any time soon and there's no need for Olivia and me to rush into anything when we've got so much going on.

I think Olivia and I knew that our relationship will probably always be up and down because we're both such strong characters and have always both taken the lead and been the dominant one in our relationships. It's tricky because of course it means you'll lock horns sometimes and it's bloody exhausting, which was one of our main issues. We'd spoken a lot about the fact that it's not right for things to be great for five or six days, and then for us to have a massive row and for it all to go to pot. It was properly draining. As much as we both wanted our relationship to go the distance, in the end it was too much stress and it's too tiring. Bickering is a pain in the arse.

Could we have changed things and made our relationship work long term? I really don't know. It's something I've thought about a lot but it's hard to put my finger on it. We talked about it and we felt like we'd tried everything, and at the end of the day there just wasn't an obvious answer.

I guess some relationships are meant to last for ever and some aren't. Sadly ours wasn't.

The break-up had been on the cards for a while because we were damaging each other. It wasn't like we fell out of love with one another and we still thought the world of each other, but one of us needed to bite the bullet and end things, and in the end that was me. We were unhappy more than we were happy so it was an obvious decision to make, but it was a really tough one. It needed to happen but we didn't want it to happen.

We'd had time apart before but nothing ever changed in that time and I came to the realisation that our relationship was heading in the wrong direction and we weren't respecting each other. We were both winding each other up and it was getting to the point of no return. Things had gone too far and too many things had been said and we couldn't pull it back.

Ending it was the right thing to do. It had been playing on my mind anyway and then when I found out that Olivia had been tweeting her ex and she'd also Facetimed him it was like the final straw. I saw the story in the papers and I messaged her saying, 'that is so disrespectful. Just don't talk to me.' She tried ringing me and I didn't answer because I was doing some rowing practice for Sports Relief, and then I didn't hear from her again. She didn't reach out to me again and I didn't contact her. After four days I was annoyed that she hadn't tried to get back in touch and apologise or explain things. It said it all really. She clearly wasn't that bothered. That's when I came to the decision that we needed to end it and move on with our lives.

I wanted to do it face to face but because of timings and the way things worked out we ended up breaking up over the phone. I'd been really upset about it and I felt so anxious about it all. All I wanted was for us to break up in the best way possible and for her to be okay. I also wanted us to be respectful to each other going forward. I didn't know how Liv would react. For all I knew she may have wanted to throw me under a bus and talk shit about me in the press. You never know how people are going to react when they're hurt and angry.

We were still contracted to film the show with ITV and we had to film the aftermath of our break up. We didn't actually break up on camera but we did film very soon afterwards and it was still very raw. Despite what people had said in the past this was the first time we had officially agreed to go our separate ways and we both knew it was for good. It wasn't a case of giving each other space and then getting back together this time. It was over.

There was never any question that we would stay together for the sake of the show. We're both too real and grounded for that. It would have been an awful thing to do. It would have been acting, and you can't act a relationship. We weren't going to gloss things up for TV and pretend it was all fine.

There was a story in the press that the show was cut from six to three episodes after the split but that wasn't the case. There was never a set amount of episodes and it was what it was. We did worry about letting down the producers but they were great about it and really understanding.

The day we filmed was horrible because I was sat in my flat waiting for Olivia to walk in and I was so nervous. The film crew were standing around so that was even more pressure. I didn't know how things were going to go down. Liv could have been in a bad mood and it could have turned horrible, or it could have gone okay. In the end it was a bit of both. We were both really on edge and emotional.

As much as neither of us wanted to, it was important for us to film the break up scene that so that there was a conclusion to it. It would have been really odd if we'd filmed a series about our relationship and then not showed something so major. We had a long chat about things after filming and we both agreed that the reasons behind the split were the right ones.

Olivia went on *Loose Woman* the following week and of course they asked her all about the break up. I knew she was going on and I thought she did really well when it must have been very hard. One of us had to break our silence and talk about it. I just wish she hadn't had to do it so soon for her sake.

It was horrible knowing that the show was going to screened and everyone was going to get this insight into our relationship when we'd broken up. Olivia and I were still feeling fragile when it aired and everyone was discussing it on social media so that was hard.

Things were tough after the break up and I was genuinely devastated. I loved Olivia and I found it really hard to adjust to life without her. I will miss spending so much time with Liv because we were like best mates as well as girlfriend and boyfriend, but I do think we'll stay in touch once things calm down and we both have a bit of space.

I think the important thing is that we both listen to ourselves and not everyone around us. None of us are the better or worse person in the break up and I plan to keep quiet about it and keep it to myself. I've cleared a lot of stuff up in this book and I think that's enough. I'm going to concentrate on keeping healthy and getting back in the gym and looking after myself.

I'm not sure whether I'll stay in the flat long term but I will be there for a little while longer because I paid a lot of rent upfront. Once the lease is up I'm seriously thinking of moving back to the Cotswolds because I'm happier there and it feels like it's where I belong. It's all I really know. I'm not making any big decisions at the moment though. I'm going to see where life takes me for a while. . .

My life goals

To get married. I'd like to go abroad and have a big wedding, and then a more traditional church wedding back home as well. I want both.

To be nice. I want to be a good person. Why would you not want that?

I want to do more riding again. I do miss it and I love it when I get to do it.

I definitely want kids. I think I'll be a well good dad.

I want to hang out with cows more. They're the best listeners.

Acknowledgements

First off, thanks so much to everyone at ITV for giving me the opportunity to take part in Love Island and go on to do all the amazing things I have, including Straight Outta Love Island and Crackin' On. If it wasn't for you none of this would be happening.

Thank you to Charlotte Hardman and everyone at Hodder for giving me the chance to tell my story. You've all been amazing to work with and it feels so good to get the truth out there. Thank you to Jordan Paramor for helping me tell my story in in the way I wanted it to be told.

Thank you to Chris and Jim at Off Limits Entertainment. I know I may not always have been your easiest client, but let's face it, I'm the most fun! Thanks for all your incredible support from day one and for steering me in the right direction.

Thank you to Mum and Dad for giving me such an amazing upbringing and continuing to support me every day, no matter how difficult I am. I know I don't say it enough but I love you both very much.

Thanks to my brilliant brothers Ben, Tom, James and Will for always being there for me (mainly when I need a pub friend).

Thanks to all my best mates, Jay, Max, Peep Show, Kem, Milb, Ceeg and Whits, who have been there through the good and bad times and never miss an opportunity to bring me back down to earth. I really have found friends for life in you lot.

A very special thanks to my fans (it feels well weird saying that. I've got fans!). You have all been incredible and whether you know it or not you've helped me through some pretty tough times. You mean the world to me.

And last, but definitely not least, thank you to Olivia for being such a huge and important part of the last year of my life. You made every day exciting and interesting, and even though we've gone our separate ways I hope we'll always be a part of each other's lives in some way.

An invitation from the publisher

Join us at www.hodder.co.uk, or follow us
on Twitter @hodderbooks to be a part of
our community of people who love the very
best in books and reading.

Whether you want to discover more about a book
or an author, watch trailers and interviews, have the
chance to win early limited editions, or simply browse
our expert readers' selection of the very best books,
we think you'll find what you're looking for.

And if you don't, that's the place to tell us what's missing.

We love what we do, and we'd love you to be a part of it.

www.hodder.co.uk

@hodderbooks

HodderBooks

HodderBooks